THE IFS OF HISTORY
How The World Might Have
Changed If Things Had Gone
Slightly Differently

THE IFS OF HISTORY
How The World Might Have Changed If Things Had Gone Slightly Differently

by

Joseph Edgar Chamberlin

Fireship Press
www.FireshipPress.com

The Ifs of History: How The World Might Have Changed If Things Had Gone Slightly Differently - Copyright © 2010 by Fireship Press

ISBN: 978-1-61179-057-3

BISAC Subject Headings:
>   HIS000000   HISTORY / General
>   HIS010000   HISTORY / Europe / General
>   HIS036000   HISTORY / United States / General

This work is based on the 1907 edition of *The Ifs of History* by Joseph Edgar Chamberlin, Philadelphia: Harry Altemus Company.

Address all correspondence to:

Fireship Press, LLC
P.O. Box 68412
Tucson, AZ 85737

Or visit our website at:
www.FireshipPress.com

1.0

Contents

PREFACE

Whether or not we believe that events are consciously ordered before their occurrence, we are compelled to admit the importance of Contingency in human affairs.

If we believe in such an orderly and predetermined arrangement, the small circumstance upon which a great event may hinge becomes, in our view, but the instrumentality by means of which the great plan is operated. It by no means sets aside the vital influence of chance to assume that "all chance is but direction which we cannot see."

For instance, the believer in special providences regards as clearly providential the flight of the flocks of birds which diverted the course of Columbus from our shores to those of the West Indies; but it is none the less true that this trivial circumstance caused the great navigator to turn his prow.

Those who, on the other hand, reject the idea of special providences, and treat history as a sequence of occurrences emerging mechanically from the relations of men with one another, must admit that causes forever contend with causes, and that the nice balance of action and reaction may sometimes be influenced radically by even so small a circumstance as the cackling of the geese of Rome. It is true that the evolutionist is apt to become a believer in necessity to an extent which appears unlikely to the mind of the other. Events, in his view, inhere in the nature and character of men, these in their turn being the result of the physical circumstances that differentiate the nations. This view seems at first to reduce the probability that accident will at any time sensibly alter the course of affairs.

But if we take historical action and reaction at their moments of equilibrium, we see that the tide of affairs may sometimes appear to follow the drift of a feather. Consider, for instance, the declaration of the Duke of Wellington that the issue of the battle of Waterloo turned upon the closing of the gates of Hugomont Castle by the hand of one man. Wellington was certainly in a position to know if this was true; and in the light of the tremendous events that depended upon the trifling act, does it not appear that accident for one moment outweighed in consequence any necessity that inhered in the character of the French people or that of the nations arrayed against them at Waterloo? It may be the function of Contingency to correct the overconfidence of the evolutionist.

At all events, we cannot dismiss the "if"; there is, as Touchstone says, much virtue in it.

J. E. C.

CHAPTER I
IF THEMISTOCLES HAD NOT BEATEN ARISTIDES IN AN ATHENIAN ELECTION

Mithra instead of Jesus? The western world Zoroastrian, not Christian?

The Persian Redeemer, always called the Light of the World in their scriptures; the helper of Ahura-Mazda, the Almighty, in his warfare with Ahriman, or Satan; the intercessor for men with the Creator; the Savior of humanity; he, Mithra, might have been the central person of the dominant religion of Europe and modern times, but for certain developments in Athenian politics in the years between 490 and 480 B. C. For it is true that in the first three of four centuries of the Christian era the western world seemed to hesitate between the religion of Mithra and that of Christ; and if the Persians had completed the conquest of Greece in the fifth century B. C., Mithra might have so strengthened his hold upon Europe that the scale would have been turned forever in his direction.

What was it that enabled the Greeks, in the crucial test, the ultimate contingency, to turn back the Persians and maintain their independence? History says that it was the result of the battles of Marathon and Salamis, in which the Greeks were triumphant over the Persians. This is true only in a limited sense. The battle of Marathon, in 490 B. C., did

1

not save Greece, for the Persians came back again more powerful than ever. At Thermopylae, Leonidas and his band died vainly, for the hosts of Xerxes overran all Greece north of the isthmus of Corinth. They took Athens, and burned the temples on the Acropolis. They were triumphant on the land.

But at Salamis, in the narrow channel between the horseshoe-shaped island and the Attica mainland, Themistocles, on the 20th day of September, 480 B. C., adroitly led the great Persian fleet of six hundred vessels into a trap and defeated it in as heroic a fight as ever the men of the West fought against the men of the East. Seated on his "throne," or rather his silver-footed chair, on a hilltop overlooking the scene, Xerxes, the master of the world, beheld the destruction of his ships, one by one, by the leagued Greeks. When the battle was over he saw that the escape of his victorious army from the mainland was imperiled, and while there was yet time, he led his Persian horde in a wild flight across his bridge of boats over the Hellespont. The field of PlatÊa completed the check, and the Persian invasions of Europe were over forever.

What was it that enabled Themistocles to win this decisive victory for Greece after disastrous defeats on land? Simply his skill in the politics of Athens. Themistocles was a Hellenic imperialist. He was opposed by Aristides, who was a very just man, and an anti-imperialist and "mugwump." Greece was at that time terribly menaced by the Persian power, and threatened with "Medization," or absorption into the Persian nationality. Themistocles saw that the country's only chance lay in a union of all the Hellenes, and in the construction of a navy worth the name. Aristides was a better orator than he, and at first won against him in the Athenian elections. The Greek spirit was innately hostile to anything like centralization or imperialism. But when Δgina, which was the leading Grecian maritime state, and had some good ships, turned against Athens and defeated it on the sea, the Athenians' eyes began to open. Themistocles pushed his plan for the construction of a fleet of two hundred vessels and the addition of twenty new ships every year to this navy.

Squarely across his path stood Aristides, with his ridicule of the attempt of little Athens to become a maritime power, and his warnings against militarism. But Themistocles, by adroit politics, led the Athenians to become sick of Aristides, and persuaded them to ostracize or banish this just man. Aristides went to Ægina. Then Themistocles rushed forward his plan of naval reform, and carried it through. The two hundred ships were built, and not a moment too soon. It was this fleet, brilliantly led by Themistocles and Eurybiades at Salamis, which entangled the Persians in the narrow waters of Salamis and defeated them, and saved Europe for the Europeans.

The victory saved it also for Christ, by keeping alive the worship of the half-gods of Greece and Rome until a whole-god came from Judea. The Persians, too, had a whole-god. Idea for idea, principle for principle, tenet for tenet, dream for dream, all of later Judaism and all of medieval Christianity, except the person and story of Jesus, was in the religion of Persia. Not only the central ideas of formal Christianity, but many of its dependent and related principles, are found in Mithraism, which was the translation of the fundamental philosophic ideas of Zoroastrianism into terms of human life. The parallel is so striking that many thinkers regard Christianity merely as Mithraism bodied forth in a story invented by, or at least told to and believed by, a circle of primitive and uneducated zealots who knew nothing of the history of the doctrines they were embracing.

But notwithstanding the philosophic likeness, the acceptance of Mithraism as it was held and practiced in Persia in Darius's time, instead of Christianity, which may have been Mithraism first Judaized and afterward Romanized, would have made a vast difference with the western world. If Greece had been Persianized before the rise of Rome's power, Rome, too, would have been Persianized. The influence of Hebrew thought upon the western world would have been forestalled. Zoroastrian rites would have prevailed. Over all would have spread the mysticism of the East.

Our civilization might have risen as high as it has ever gone, in art, in the grace of life; but instead of being inspired with the eager desire of progress, by the restless Hellenic necessity of doing something better and higher, or at least something other, something new—instead of this, the spirit of peace and of satisfaction with old ideals would have permeated our systems and our life.

Lord Mithra, too, would have been primarily the sun, primarily an embodiment of the light shining down to us through the sky from that central essence which alone can say, "I am that I am," and not, as in the Lord Christ, a humble, suffering, poor and despised man lifted up into Godhead.

CHAPTER II
IF THE MOORS HAD WON
THE BATTLE OF TOURS

The most tremendous contingencies in all history—the determination of the fate of whole continents, whole civilizations, by a single incident—are sometimes the occurrences that are most completely and signally ignored by the ordinary citizen. For instance, it does not occur to the man on the street that but for a turn in the tide of battle on a certain October day in the year 732, on a sunny field in northern-central France, he, the man on the street, would today be a devout Mussulman, listening at evening for the muezzin's call from a neighboring minaret, abjuring pork and every alcoholic beverage, and shunning stocks and all kinds of speculation as prohibited forms of gambling.

Islamism would today, but for a single hard-fought battle and its issue, probably be the established form of religion in all Europe. Even England would have been unable to resist the onset of the impetuous Arabs, once they had established themselves in triumph from the Tagus to the Vistula; and the conversion of all Europe would have carried with it the Moslemization of the new world—supposing, indeed, that America had up to this time been discovered under Moorish auspices, which is unlikely.

The Ifs of History

Europe was certainly nearer to conquest by the Moors in the eighth century than most people suppose. There are few finer or more heroic episodes in history than the extraordinary series of conquests by means of which, a handful of fanatical Arabs, inspired by the prophet Mohammed, carried, with fire and sword, the faith of Islam over the world, until, within two hundred years of the date of the prophet's birth, it reigned from the shores of the Atlantic to the banks of the Indus. Horde after horde of impetuous warriors of the Crescent had arisen. Their purpose, frankly, was to convert the world, and convert it by force. Cutting themselves off from their bases of supply, and relying upon an alliance of miracle and rapine to sustain them, their triumphant campaigns were one continuous and colossal Sherman's march to the sea.

They struck Europe at the east, and also by way of the west. Greek fire checked them at the gates of Constantinople in the east, but they overran all northern Africa, crossed the Straits of Gibraltar, and flowed like a torrent over Spain and southern France. By the year 731, as Gibbon truly says, the whole south of France, from the mouth of the Garonne to that of the Rhone, had assumed the manners and religion of Arabia.

Abd-er-Rahman, the conqueror, reigned supreme in southwestern Europe. Spain and Portugal had been annexed to Asia, and now the turn of France had surely come.

But at this crisis a heroic figure arose in Europe—scarcely an elegant figure, though a picturesque one. The throne of the Franks had been seized by an illegitimate son of old King Pepin, a rough and heedless fighter, whose rule pleased the people better than did that of the priests and women whom Pepin had left behind him. This bloody-handed usurper was named Charles, or Karl, and he was destined afterward to be called Martel, "the Hammer," on account of the iron blows that he struck upon all who faced him.

Abd-er-Rahman, the victorious Moor, advanced into northern France, overthrowing armies with ease, and sacking cities, churches and convents as he marched. Nothing could stay him, as it appeared. He had planted the standard of the prophet at the gates of Tours, which is one hundred and thirty miles, as the crow flies, from Paris. But meantime the usurping and base-born Charles, in command of a small army mostly composed of gigantic and well-seasoned German warriors, was sneaking along, like an Indian, under the shelter of a range of hills, toward the Saracen camp; and one day, to Abd-er-Rahman's great surprise, Charles fell upon him like a veritable hammer of red-hot iron.

Not in one moment, nor in one day, was the issue decided. Six days the armies fought, and through all Abd-er-Rahman and his fanatical horde held their own. But on the seventh day Charles led a battalion of his biggest, fiercest Germans straight against the Moorish center. Abd-er-Rahman himself was slain; his army, appalled by this circumstance, was broken and beaten, and faded away toward the South.

Charles Martel made sure his victory by another successful campaign. The Moors were driven out of France forever. In their stead Charles himself reigned. He had saved Europe to Christianity. Yet for his lack of docility, the church execrated him.

If Abd-er-Rahman had overrun France, as he would surely have done if a less redoubtable and terrible antagonist than Charles Martel had faced him at Tours, he would next have turned his attention to Germany. With its fall, Italy and Rome would have invited his attention. There he would have found few but priests to oppose him, and the empire of the East, attacked in the rear as well as in the front, would speedily have succumbed. No Saint Cyril would have gone forth to convert the Russians and Bulgarians, who would promptly have been Tartarized.

As we have seen, nothing could have saved England or Ireland. The prophet's world-conquest must have been accomplished.

The Ifs of History

What then? Would the western world have remained at the stage of cultivation in which we see Arabia today? There is no reason to suppose that that would have been quite the case. It was not so in Moorish Spain, which rose to a high level of culture. Christianity would not have been suppressed. It was not suppressed in Turkey or Spain. But it would probably have been ruled, dominated, forced into odd corners, and to some extent Moslemized. Learning would not have languished, for in certain important forms it flourished in Spain. The western brain, the Aryan genius, must have had its way in many intellectual respects. Yet the cast of European thought would surely have been sicklied over with oriental contemplativeness.

The "hustler" never could have existed under Moslem rule. The speculator never would have risen, because he would not have been tolerated. The Moslem doctrine forbids censuses and statistics, treating them as a form of wicked curiosity concerning the rule of God on earth. Pictorial art, and sculpture, which the Koran regards as idolatrous, would have been sternly repressed. Literature would have been great along the line of poetry; science great along the line of mathematics.

The western woman would have been orientalized. So far from forming clubs, she would not have been permitted even to pray in the mosques.

America would have remained undiscovered for centuries; and if at last accident or search had laid it bare, it would have followed the path of Europe. The mellifluous tones of the muezzin's cadence, "*La ilah 'i il 'Allah*," "There is no god but God," would echo now where the shouts and yells of the Wall Street speculators reverberate. And the abode of the mighty would have been a House of Quiet, not the home of strenuousness.

CHAPTER III
IF KING ETHELRED OF ENGLAND HAD NOT MARRIED THE NORMAN EMMA

Not much turns upon the marriage of kings in these days. The German Kaiser is not the less German assuredly because his mother was an Englishwoman. Nor did her marriage to the Crown Prince of Prussia give Prussia or Germany the slightest hold upon England.

It was altogether different in an earlier day. One royal marriage in particular, that of King Ethelred the Redeless, the "Unready," of England, to Emma, the daughter of Richard the Fearless, Duke of Normandy, in the year 1002, exercised upon Britain and the world the most tremendous influence. It led to the invasion and subjugation of England by William, surnamed the Conqueror, and to the reconstruction of that mother country of ours, politically, socially and racially, upon new lines. No royal marriage, perhaps, ever had such enduring and far-reaching consequences; no queen-elect ever took with her to her adopted country such a lading of fateful changes.

The marriage was a sufficiently commonplace affair in itself. Ethelred was a smooth and rather gentle prince, who thought much more of his own easy fortunes than of anything else. He wanted a wife, and he did not like the Danes, who were racially and politically the nearest neighbors of his royal house. He visited Normandy, and must have pleased the Duke, for Richard, a bold and resourceful man, bestowed this fair-haired Emma, a lineal descendant of the victorious Norse pirates, but now quite Frenchified, upon the young Englishman.

She was not destined to see her progeny long reign over England. But it did not matter about her descendants. The great change did not come with them. What she really did was to supply to her nephew, Duke William, known to history as the Conqueror, who was yet to come to the throne of Normandy, a pretext to seize the English crown for himself.

William was of illegitimate birth. His mother was Arvela, a poor girl whom Duke Robert saw washing clothes in the river one day and straightway became enamored of. But on his father's side William was, through Emma's marriage, cousin of King Edward the Confessor, son of the unready Ethelred. On a lucky day for him he visited England. It was at a time when Edward was very ill, and William claimed ever after that he had received from Edward, on his sick bed, a solemn promise that the Norman duke should succeed him upon the English throne.

Edward had no son, but it appears quite unlikely that a wise ruler such as he was should deliberately have given away the throne and country to a foreigner, especially when his brother-in-law Harold, Earl of Wessex, a capable man, stood ready to succeed him. The English, at any rate, took this view of the matter, for they straightway made Harold king, ignoring the claim of the vilely born Duke William to the throne.

But as the world knows, William was able to make good his flimsy claim. Whether Edward gave him the crown or not, Stamford Bridge and Hastings did give it him. When at last, following the law of the time, he presented himself to the suffrage of the English nation, the representatives of the beaten people had no option but to elect him. He was a part of the baggage that Queen Emma brought with her.

What was the rest of it? For one thing, union and con-solidation, centralization. England up to that time had been but a broken congeries of earldoms or tribal territories, and would have gone on thus if it had not at last found a master. In the next place, William brought the touch of France, of Rome, of the graceful Latin world, to England. This son of a hundred pirates passed on to England the torch of a culture that had been lighted in Greece and reignited in Rome. It was not for nothing that what had been ox meat with the Saxons now became beef for the English; what had been calves' flesh became veal, and base swine flesh reappeared as a more elegant dish called pork. It meant something that the rude language of Beowulf was to be succeeded by the smoother lilt of Chaucer—that, in short, the English had a new and bookish tongue.

It meant, in simple truth, the disappearance of the old England and the birth of a new and greater nation. "It was in these years of subjection," says Green, "that England became really England." The Normans degraded the bulk of the Eng-lish lords, but they made these displaced nobles the nucleus of a new middle class. At the same time their protection led to the elevation into the same middle class of a race of culti-vators who had been peasants. Furthermore, the Norman rule expanded villages into towns and cities, and these in time began to stand, as powerful boroughs, for the rights of the people. The conquest, says Green, "secured for England a new communion with the artistic and intellectual life of the world without her. To it we owe not merely English wealth and English freedom, but England herself."

Edward A. Freeman calls the Norman conquest "the most important event in English history since the first coming of the English and their conversion to Christianity." If the suc-cession of native kings had continued, says the same author-ity, "freedom might have died out step by step, as it did in some other lands. As it was, the main effect of the conquest was to call out the ancient English spirit in a new and an-tagonistic shape, to give the English nation new leaders in the conquerors who were gradually changed into country-men, and by the union of the men of both races, to win back the substance of the old institutions under new forms."

In other words, the Norman Princess Emma brought with her John Bull as a part of her dowry, when she came to weak Ethelred as his bride.

CHAPTER IV
IF COLUMBUS HAD KEPT HIS
COURSE STRAIGHT WESTWARD

On the morning of the 7th day of October, 1492, Christopher Columbus, sailing unknown seas in quest of "Cipango," the Indies, and the Grand Khan, still held resolutely to a course which he had laid out due to the westward. This course he held in spite of the murmurings of his crew, who wished to turn back, and contrary to the advice of that skilled and astute navigator, Martin Alonzo Pinzon, who commanded the *Pinta*. Pinzon had repeatedly advised that the course be altered to the southwestward.

Columbus was sailing on a theory. Pinzon, like any other practical navigator in a strange sea, was feeling his way, and answering the indications of the waters, the skies, the green grasses that drifted on the surface of the waves, the flocks of birds that wheeled, and dipped, and showed their heels to the far-wandered navigators, and seemed to know their way so well over that remote and uncharted wilderness of the deep. Columbus had said, "We will sail to the west, and ever to the west, until the west becomes the east." Which to the men before the mast was sheer lunacy. But Pinzon had already found strange Afric lands. The scent of their leaves and flowers seemed to lie in his nostrils.

13

The Ifs of History

Martin Alonzo Pinzon put off in a boat, later on that 7th day of October, and came back to the *Santa Maria,* in which was the Admiral. He brought the information that he had seen "a great multitude of birds passing from the north to the southwest; from which cause he deemed it reasonable to suppose that they (the birds) were going to sleep on land, or were perhaps flying from winter which must be approaching in the countries from which they came." The Admiral knew it was by the aid of the flight of birds that the Portuguese had discovered the greater part of the new lands which they had found. Columbus hesitated, wavered.

Had the heart of the great theorist, sailing obstinately straight west in obedience to the call of the land whose presence there he had reasoned out, misgiven him at last? Had the discouragement and incredulity of his men affected him? We do not know. But we do know that finally he heeded Pinzon's oft-repeated demand that the course be altered.

It looked like common sense to follow the birds. Really it was not. The theory was his true guide. Columbus betrayed his faith; he resolved, as his journal recorded, "to turn his prow to the west-southwest, with the determination of pursuing that course *for two days.*" He never resumed the westward course. He had weakened in his devotion to his own idea—and had lost a continent for Spain and the Roman Catholic Church.

For in spite of the conclusion reached by John Boyd Thacher, in his monumental work on Columbus, that even if the Admiral had held the westward course his fleet would not have passed the northernmost tip of the Bahamas, there is sufficient ground for the generally accepted conclusion that his landfall in that case would have been on the coast of Florida or South Carolina, or even North Carolina. After the alteration of his course, Columbus continued to sail for four days in a general southwesterly direction, before, on the 12th of October, he fell upon Watling's Island. In that time he had sailed, according to his own reckoning, one hundred and forty-one leagues. This distance, if persisted in due to the westward, would have brought him in contact with drift and real bird-flight indications of the continent.

Let us see toward what point his course had been laid. Setting sail from Gomera, in the Canary Islands, Columbus purposed to go straight to the west until he reached land. Gomera lies in about the latitude of Cape Canaveral, or the Indian River, Florida. A line drawn from Gomera to Cape Canaveral passes to the northward of the Bahamas altogether. No land lay in the Admiral's path to Florida.

But any supposition that Columbus would not have gone to the northward of the Indian River ignores the northward drift that the Gulf Stream would have caused his ships. He had yet, of course, to reach the axis of that powerful current, which is here comparatively narrow, and runs very swiftly at the point where the due westward course from Gomera would have struck it. It is a fair chance that this drift would have carried Columbus so far north as to land him in the neighborhood of what is now Charleston, S. C., or even further to the northward, if he had followed the path he had laid out for himself.

Amazing the consequences that hung upon the flight of those "multitudes of birds" that wheeled Bahama-ward on that October day! The Admiral's landfall on the coast even of Florida would have made all temperate America Spanish, for it would have focused the might of Ferdinand and Isabella upon our shores. We know that the islands which lay immediately to the southward of his "Salvador," in the Bahamas, beckoned Columbus in that direction, and that the Indians were able by signs to make it clear to him that a greater land, which was Cuba, and which he called "Cipango," lay in this southerly direction. That way he laid his course, "in order," as he wrote in his journal, "to go to this other island which is very large and where all these men whom I am bringing from the island of San Salvador make signs that there is a great deal of gold and that they wear bracelets of it on their arms and legs and in their ears and in their noses and on their breasts."

Reason enough! Only it meant that Spain's energy in this hemisphere was to be directed to the West Indies, and South America, and Mexico, for as long a time as it was destined to endure, and that the vast continental North was to be left as the heritage of another race.

It is true that Florida afterward became Spanish. But it was not a question of what Florida, merely, was to be. If Columbus had landed upon the mainland, the northeastward trend of the coast, reaching back toward Spain by just so much, would have beckoned him northward, not southward. Even if he had explored southwardly, by some chance, he must have returned northward when he had reached the point of the Florida peninsula; and in the northerly direction he would have cruised, returning Europe-ward. And he would have annexed the land step by step, as he annexed Cuba, Hispaniola, and all the southern lands as fast as he touched them.

The Carolinas, Virginia, Maryland, would have been the scenes of the Spaniards' settlement for a hundred years. Though afterward they took Florida, that was as a mere side issue; it was unconsidered, neglected, after Cuba and Mexico; and was passed on at length to the race that came to the mainland more than a hundred years after the landfall at San Salvador.

Who can estimate the consequences of a fate which should have sent Columbus straight on his way! Who can compass the thought of the millions of country-loving Americans of our race unborn here, but nurtured under skies now foreign to their very nature, but for that glittering flock of tropical birds whirling southwestwardly? It is no idle conjecture; von Humboldt, one of the wisest of cosmographers, says that never in the world's history had the flight of birds such momentous consequences. "It may be said," he avers, "to have determined the first settlements in the new continent, and its distribution between the Latin and Germanic races." He believed that the Gulf Stream would have carried

16

Columbus around Cape Hatteras. It might indeed have done so.

We of the United States may well believe that the hand of Providence guided those birds on that October day; but none the less are we compelled to admit the strange dependence of human events upon circumstances that are most trifling in themselves.

CHAPTER V
IF QUEEN ELIZABETH I HAD
LEFT A SON OR DAUGHTER

Never did greater events hinge upon a woman's caprice against marriage than those which were poised on the will of Elizabeth I, Queen of England, in the long years that lay between the time when, as a young queen, it was proposed to marry her to the Duke of Anjou, and the sere and yellow leaf of her womanhood, when her potential maternity was past.

If Elizabeth had married, as her people often implored her to do, and if her progeny had sat upon the throne and continued the sway of the Tudors, half a century of turmoil and bloodshed, under the essentially foreign rule of the Stuarts, might have been spared to England. The Revolution doubtless would never have taken place. The material and intellectual advance of England and all Britain would have been steady and sure upon the splendid foundation of the Elizabethan structure.

But, on the other hand, as good is often evolved from evil, much that is sacred and vital to the whole Anglo-Saxon race might have been missed. The Bill of Rights, the Habeas Corpus Act and other guarantees that were obtained through the Revolution or the Commonwealth would have been wanting in the English Constitution. Oliver Cromwell and John

Hampden would probably have remained in rustic obscurity. All modern Europe would have lacked the political incentive, the revolutionary impulse, the constructive audacity, which it has derived from the Grand Remonstrance, from the battle-fields of Marston Moor and Naseby, where royalty was overthrown by the arm of the common people, and from the eternal menace that lay in the death-block of King Charles.

It was not because of any aversion to the society of men that Elizabeth remained unmarried. Very far from this; it is likely that her extreme liking for male society cut a considerable figure in her refusal. She did not propose to give any man a public right to interfere with her liberty of choice in this regard. History agrees that there was a sting of truth in the words of Mary, Queen of Scots, in a letter which she once sent to Elizabeth: "Your aversion to marriage proceeds from your not wishing to lose the liberty of compelling people to make love to you." The queen was fickle and passionate. She had little fear of the royal Mrs. Grundy. At the tender age of sixteen scandal linked her name with that of the Lord Admiral Seymour in such a way that an investigation by the council was necessary. She baffled the lawyers in the examination by her "very good wit."

From the time of her accession, at the age of twenty-five, to the time of her death, Elizabeth was certainly never without a favorite. She had small conscience, and there can be little doubt that she required the assassination of poor Amy Robsart in order that her favorite, Dudley, might be free from his young wife; and when, after the age of sixty, her young cavalier of that time, the fascinating Essex, wearying of dancing attendance upon her at court, joined the expedition of Drake against Portugal, the Queen bade him return instantly at his "uttermost peril." In the end she signed the unhappy Essex's death warrant for an alleged rebellion against her.

But her motive in refusing matrimony was not altogether—perhaps not even chiefly—one of coquetry. She was avid of power, and could brook no rival in its exercise. It is probable that considerations of real patriotism restrained her from marrying a continental prince. She shrank from introducing foreign influence as instinctively as Americans have at all times. She shrank from bowing to any yoke of Europe. But there were also objections to her marrying an Englishman. If she had chosen one she would have aroused the jealousy of all Englishmen not of his party or following. She regarded it as the better policy to keep them all hoping.

The unmarried state suited her arrogant and domineering nature well. She had none of the docility which made Queen Victoria a model house-wife and mother, and also a model constitutional sovereign. It was her purpose to have undivided power or none. To the deputation of the House of Commons which visited her with a petition that she marry, she answered: "For me it shall be sufficient that a marble stone declare that a queen, having reigned such a time, lived and died a virgin."

The Commons who uttered the petition must have felt a premonition of what would actually take place if there were no heir of Elizabeth's body. The next heir to the throne was Mary, Queen of Scots. She was a zealous Catholic, and England had just fully established its religious independence. It is true that Mary's son and heir, James, who afterward became King of England, as well as of Scotland, was a Protestant, but the loyalty of the adhesion of his house to the new confession might well have been distrusted. There was no promise of happiness for England in the accession of a prince or princess of this house to its throne.

But the Stuarts came—and the troubles of England began in real earnest. Elizabeth's reign had been, as it then seemed to all Englishmen, and as in very many respects it was, the golden age of Britain. Never had art, and literature, and material prosperity, risen to so high a level. The world seemed opening to a new and glorious life, like a rose bursting into bloom. In literature it had been the age of Shakespeare and Bacon. But with the Stuarts, literature and art passed into a long eclipse. Shakespeare's light may be said to have gone out for a hundred years, to be lighted again only from the borrowed torch of German culture.

Let us suppose that Elizabeth had been able to find a consort as wise and as harmless as was Prince Albert, the husband of Queen Victoria. Let us suppose that the pair had left behind them a thoroughly English prince, their own son, a man who would have been capable of continuing Elizabeth's prudent rule and of holding England to its traditions while maintaining the extraordinary advance that had marked her splendid reign. Without James's mingled poltroonery and tyranny to nurse and stimulate it, it is doubtful if Puritanism would have had its spasm of ascendency. English history would have been spared an epoch of chaos, of wild experimentation, of political empirics.

At the same time it would have been deprived of a form of political genius which was hammered out of the fire of rebellion. English Whiggism, English liberalism, English nonconformity have made the world over anew. America, in particular, would have been infinitely poorer without the Puritan ferment. Should we have had the New England migration at all, if England had continued its calm and homogeneous development under Elizabethan influences? Would not rather all America have been like Virginia, and the new world organized on a roast-beef, plum-pudding and distinctly Anglican and conformist basis?

If we can imagine Massachusetts a purely Episcopal colony today, ruled by parochial vestries instead of by town-meeting-parliaments and the village Gladstone and his responsible cabinet in every hamlet, and the whole province presided over by some self-sufficient Sir Alexander Swettenham as the representative of British royalty, we may perhaps imagine England without the cataclysm of the Stuarts.

CHAPTER VI
IF THE PHILARMONIA HAD
NOT GIVEN CONCERTS AT VICENZA

For the sake of variety, perhaps of diversion, in the midst of more serious speculations, let us have an "if" of musical history—and one which, no doubt, musicians may regard as purely fanciful, totally absurd. It should be stated at the start that this chapter is written by one who has no knowledge of music, but is capable of a very keen enjoyment of it, and has in his time heard much professional music—many concerts, operas and oratorios—and also much of the spontaneous untrained music of the people, including old New England ballads now forgotten; the songs of German peasants at the fireside and spinning wheel; the native corn songs, "wails" and "shouts" of Southern negroes on the plantations; and the medicine songs, scalp songs, ceremonial chants and love ditties of the American Indians.

The contingency which will be presented here is this: If a certain group of unprofessional singers and musicians in the highly cultivated Italian town of Vicenza, about midway of the sixteenth century, had not banded themselves together in a society called the Philarmonia, and for the first time in Europe given musical entertainments to which the public were admitted, the musical institution called the concert might never have existed, and music in that case would have remained a spontaneous expression of human emotion, untainted with what is now called virtuosity—that is, the strife and strain after technical mastery, which affects the whole character of music, and diverts it from its original purpose of pleasing the sense and comforting the heart.

Expert professional music was a thing of very slow growth. The old chapelmasters or choirmasters were, of course, in a sense professional, since they lived upon the church. But they had also a sacerdotal character. At the beginning they were always priests. To make a class of professional musicians, vying with one another for mere mastery, the public concert, with paid musicians, had to be developed.

Though the Philarmonia gave public concerts at Vicenza, as we have said, in the middle of the sixteenth century, concert music and opera music had no general existence for as much as a century afterward. The first opera ever represented was Peri's "Eurydice," written about 1600. Even that was merely the expression of a group of enthusiasts, a sort of private attempt to embody a theory of their own about what music should be. It was not until the year 1672 that the first concert, with a price for admission, was given in London. The price then charged was a shilling, and the concert was in a private house.

By that time the start had been made. Other concerts were given soon afterward. They became popular. There was a demand for skilled musicians and soloists. Performers began practicing for the sake of excelling in technical achievement. By swift and sudden steps a premium was put upon mechanical perfection in the handling of instruments. The old spontaneous methods of expression gradually became discredited.

As a consequence of the new development, two sorts of music grew up in the world. On the one side stood concert music, professional music, virtuoso music. This was difficult and complicated, and it was impossible for ordinary people to sing it or play it. On the other side was the popular music—folk music, the music of the street, the nursery, the stable-shed and the taproom. As popular music was regularly deserted now for the concert school by those who possessed the greatest musical talent, it began to degenerate until it reached at last the degradation of "Grandfather's Clock," "Ta-ra-ra-boom-de-ay," "Waiting at the Church" and the graphophone.

On the other hand, concert music moved farther and farther away from the hearts and the comprehension of the people, until it has become a thing apart from their lives, to be enjoyed almost as much with the eye as with the ear, the interest lying chiefly in the production, in succession, of individual masters, each of whom visibly surpasses the mechanical achievements of his immediate predecessor.

If those first concerts had not been given by the Philarmonia at Vicenza, and the idea had not slowly rippled outward thence, like spreading circles from a stone thrown into the water, until it reached Vienna, Paris and London, what would have been the state of music today?

Manifestly the development of church music would have gone on. The people, no doubt, would have been taking part in magnificent chorals. The masses of the Catholic Church would have their correspondent feature in the anthems and hymns sung in the Protestant churches by the congregations. Every instrument that existed in the sixteenth century would have been perfected, but not one would have taken on the intricate development which musical mechanism exacts.

In other words, the harpsichord would never have become a piano, and the electrical church organ would not have been heard of. We should all play some such instrument as the harp, the violin, the viol, the flute, the pipe or the dulcimer. All might have been composers, as the negroes and Indians are today, but on a higher plane.

What popular music might be now but for that unlucky Philarmonia discovery is suggested by an extract from the writings of Thomas Morley, an Englishman who became a great amateur and introducer of Italian madrigals in his own country. In the year 1597 he wrote that, on a certain evening, in England,—

> ...supper being ended, and musicke-bookes, according to the custome, being brought to the table, the mistresse of the house presented mee with a part, earnestly requesting mee to sing. But when, after manie excuses, I protested unfainedly that I could not, euerie one began to wonder. Yea, some whispered unto others, demanding how I was brought up. So that, upon shame of mine ignorance, I go now to seek out mine old friende master Gnorimus, to make myselfe his schollar.

In those days a person who could not sing, and sing well, was regarded as a freak, and was required to fit himself to join in the universal diversion. If we had not turned over our music making to professionals it would be so now. Instead of going to the concert or the opera after the evening meal, or playing bridge or talking scandal, people would have participated in the singing of madrigals, glees or whatever other sort of popular spontaneous music had been developed, and all would have been sustained and uplifted by the exalted joy that comes from joining with others in the production of good music.

The people would have been joyously and heartily musical. Their taste would not have been degraded to the point where it is gratified, as in the graphophone, with a complicated succession of flat and strident sounds unmusical in themselves.

CHAPTER VII
IF THE SPANISH ARMADA HAD
SAILED WHEN IT WAS SUPPOSED TO

When Philip the Second, son of the great emperor Charles V, came to the throne of Spain, that country had become the greatest cosmopolitan empire in the world. The throne of Castile, at one time or another during Philip's reign, was the throne not only of Spain and Portugal, but of the Netherlands and Burgundy, the Sicilies, Sardinia, Milan, Cuba, Hispaniola, Florida, Mexico, California, nearly all of South America, and the Philippine Islands. The Spanish monarch was the eldest son of the church; and Philip, strong, ambitious, bigoted and insolent, expected, as he laid the foundations of his glorious palace, the Escorial, the eighth wonder of the world, to become master of France and Britain, and to bequeath to his son the vastest empire that the sun had ever shone upon.

By his marriage with Queen Mary he acquired the nominal title of king of England, though he was never crowned. But his grudge rose against England after Mary's death and Elizabeth's accession. The country proved itself a thorn in his side, helping the Dutch rebels and undoing at home the persecuting work of his late spouse. Philip formed a great project for the invasion of the country.

The Ifs of History

Spain was supreme then on the sea. The English navy had greatly declined. In 1575 it had but twenty-four vessels of all classes on the water. Philip knew the cleverness of the English with their ships, however, and in planning this invasion he proposed to be invincible. Invincible he sought to make the Armada, or fleet, that he sent against the country, and invincible not only he, but all Europe, believed it to be, when, in January of the year 1588, the great flotilla was ready to sail.

It consisted of about one hundred and thirty ships, of which sixty-two were over three hundred tons burden. It was commanded by a brave and skillful sea fighter, Santa Cruz. The English had bettered their conditions of seven years before very greatly, but they were at this moment absolutely unprepared to meet a foreign fleet. Their ships were scattered far and wide, and many were unequipped. If the Armada had sailed at that moment it would have found no force ready to meet it. And it would have escaped the storms that later befell.

But *mañana* is the curse of all Spain's projects. The Armada lingered. Santa Cruz, its chief, sickened in port and died. Very likely if he had sailed no such fate would have overtaken him. This was the first of the big fleet's misfortunes. Philip looked about for another commander. By a fatuous favoritism his choice fell upon the Duke of Medina Sidonia, who was utterly incompetent.

The months flew past. Meantime the English, fully apprised of the king's intentions, were getting a fleet together. In those days it was not necessary to wait five years for a battleship to be constructed. Almost any big ship could be turned into a fighting craft. In particular, the English were well off in guns, and the delay of the Armada gave them a chance to get their artillery on board.

When—*nombre de Dios!*—does the reader suppose that this invincible fleet, ready in January, really set sail from Coruña? On the 12th day of July! It had already been scattered and weakened by a storm off Lisbon. On the 21st of July

Medina Sidonia sailed into Drake's and Hawkins's "line ahead" formation in the English channel as Rojestvensky sailed into Togo's lair off Tsu-Shima in 1905, and the result to him somewhat resembled the subsequent fate of the Russian fleet in the Sea of Japan. It was not, however, so bad. If Medina Sidonia had gone, with his surviving ships, after the first onset, to Denmark, and refitted, he might yet have embarrassed the British. But he sought to make the passage around the north of Scotland, and a succession of storms wrecked his whole remaining fleet.

All authorities agree that in January, 1588, no English force existed which could have hoped to check Santa Cruz as things then stood. What if he had come on and landed an army of trained veterans upon England's undefended shores? He must have won. Queen Elizabeth must have been overthrown. Ireland would have gladly joined Philip. England was almost half Catholic, and the people of that faith might eventually have become reconciled to the foreigner. Philip might have made himself another Norman William. The Spanish culture would have been imposed upon the English nation. But unlike William of Normandy, who transferred his power to Britain, Philip would have remained a Spanish sovereign, and London would have been ruled from Madrid.

Philip would never have temporized with English Protestantism. The chances are that he would have stamped it out utterly and at the start, as he sought, too late, to do in the Netherlands. If he might have worked his will, he would also have suppressed English learning and literature. William Shakespeare, who had just come up to London, had never produced a play when the Armada sailed, and probably he never would have produced one if it had conquered. The glorious Elizabethan culture would have been nipped in the bud.

All Britain's possessions in the new world, already existent or to be, would have fallen to Spain or France if Philip had overthrown Elizabeth—doubtless to Spain, for Philip's ambition to seize the French throne would have been furthered by his conquest of England. Spanish viceroys would have borne sway for centuries over all North America. A hybrid Indian-Latin race would have arisen here, as in Mexico and Peru. Lacking the inspiration of North American freedom, all Spanish America to the southward would have remained to this day under the dons.

Castilian speech, Castilian cultivation, Castilian manners, the Castilian faith, might have reigned supreme over a dusky race from the St. Lawrence to the Straits of Magellan.

CHAPTER VIII
IF CHAMPLAIN HAD TARRIED
IN PLYMOUTH BAY

On the 18th of July, in the year 1605, Samuel de Champlain, in command of a ship of the King of France, and engaged in the search for an eligible site for a great settlement, anchored in the harbor which was afterward to be known as the harbor of Plymouth, in New England. Two days before, he had been in Boston Bay. He mapped both these havens, and expressed his approval of the physical resources, and also the native Indian peoples, of the region.

At that time the coast of New England was really unappropriated, though soon after it was claimed by both France and England. It was merely a question which power should first seriously undertake the settlement of the country. If France planted her colony here, the land was destined to be French. If England hers, it would be English.

Champlain carefully studied the advantages of Boston and Plymouth. That he thought favorably of the latter place is proved by the very decent map, still extant, which he made of Plymouth and Duxbury waters. "Port St. Louis," he called the place, after the patron saint of France, and after his royal master. It looked very much as if he hoped that the spot he so honored would be made the seat of the French empire in the western world.

But Champlain sailed away, bearing with him the blessing of the thickly settled and sedentary native people. He passed around Cape Cod, and went westward as far as Nauset harbor, near New Bedford. And then, in due time, he sailed for France. When, in 1608, he finally laid the foundations of the city which was to be the capital of France in the new world, he did not lay them at Plymouth or Boston, but at Quebec, on the St. Lawrence.

Why was his choice thus made? Largely, no doubt, because Champlain, whose accurate information and seemingly always wise observation were greatly trusted by the King of France, was infatuated with the noble aspect and vast proportions of the gulf and river of St. Lawrence. He was first of all a sailor, and he had seen nothing to compare with the magnificence of this great *embouchure*. Here were scope and refuge for the greatest of navies! Here, it seemed, was a place designed by the Almighty to be the seat of an empire!

Champlain had an excellent eye for harbors, but not so good an eye of prophecy for the grand constructive events that were to be. He left the Massachusetts coast unappropriated. First its native inhabitants, so numerous, so gentle, so industrious, were decimated by a plague that came to them from the white men. Only a remnant survived. And when, in 1620, their sachem, Samoset, shouted "Welcome, Englishmen!" to the men of the Mayflower, the Indian king hailed, unconsciously, the advent of an empire which was to cast the domain of New France into a cold and waning shadow. For Quebec was too far north, and its hinterland too poor and restricted, ever to nurse an imperial race.

What if Champlain had been more sagacious, and had made his stand on the coast of Massachusetts? In all probability the settlement would have been definitive. The Pilgrims of Plymouth and the Puritans of Boston, finding no place for their settlement in the north, would, in 1620, have gone to Virginia or Georgia. The steely Yankee wedge which, on one side, was to force the Dutch out of New Amsterdam, and on the other the French out of Port Royal and Acadia, would never have been driven. New England would have been French forever, and New York Dutch.

The principle of the hinterland was asserted so successfully in our early history that Massachusetts and Connecticut were able to claim territory as far west as the Mississippi River. It was by means of this hinterland claim that the young American republic succeeded in rounding out its northwestern possessions, after the War of the Revolution, and obtaining Ohio, Indiana, Michigan, Wisconsin and Illinois. All these would have been French if Champlain had made New England French; and the English colonies, if they had ever become strong enough to throw off the British yoke, would have consisted of a restricted section in the Southeast.

Indeed, without Sam Adams, Otis, Warren, and Israel Putnam, without the revolt against the Stamp Act, and without Lexington, Concord and Bunker Hill, it is impossible to conceive of the American republic at all.

Supposing it to have been constituted notwithstanding, it would have had to do without the influence of the New England town meeting, the New England common free school, the New England college, and the congregational system of church organization. It would have been deprived of the work of Franklin, Hancock, the Adamses, Webster, Sumner, Garrison, Phillips, Grant and the Shermans, in its affairs, and of Longfellow, Emerson, Holmes, Lowell, Whittier, Hawthorne and Parkman in its intellectual life.

What would the New England country and the people have been like, if Champlain had never turned back from Plymouth Bay? We know from Benjamin Franklin's account what the progeny of the English settlers had become even as long ago as 1772. "I thought often," he wrote in that year, "of the happiness of New England, where every man is a freeholder, has a vote in public affairs, lives in a tidy, warm house, has plenty of good food and fuel, with whole clothes from head to foot, the manufacture perhaps of his own family. Long may they continue in this situation!" What the Canadian habitant is today, we know. Very often he is unable to read or write, and his material and moral condition very low. Even as late as 1837 the Canadian provinces were still arbitrarily ruled by royal governors, with appointed councils or upper houses which had a veto on all legislation. There was no self-rule, and the mass of the French people were illiterate and miserably poor.

Sieur Samuel de Champlain did a good day's work for English-speaking America, and the great free republic that was to be, when he pointed his prow northward and sailed away, out of sight of Cape Cod, in the summer of 1605.

CHAPTER IX
IF CHARLES II HAD ACCEPTED
THE KINGSHIP OF VIRGINIA

Once at least the New World has furnished to the Old World a reigning, actual king; once, for thirteen years, a monarch, sitting on a throne in America, ruled thence an ancient kingdom in Europe. And twice this singular thing might have happened, with this time an enthroned sovereign on the banks of the James instead of on the shore of a Brazilian bay, if a certain king's son and king-to-be had been of a somewhat more venturing and less indolent disposition.

The occasion when the thing really happened was when Don John VI, King of Portugal, removed his royal throne and all the paraphernalia of government from Lisbon to Rio de Janeiro, in 1807 (being impelled thereto by an intrusive movement on the part of one Napoleon Bonaparte), and turned Portugal (after the withdrawal of the French) into an actual dependency of Brazil. This it remained until King John recrossed the Atlantic in 1820. Throughout that period the scepter bore sway from west to east, from America Europe-ward.

Very much the same thing would have occurred further north in the contingency to which I have referred; and if it had, a royalist or monarchist influence might have been laid upon the English colonies in America which would have colored their history and institutions in a marked degree, even if their destiny had not been permanently affected.

When Charles I, King of England, was arrested, imprisoned, and put to death by the Parliament party in 1649, Virginia experienced a shock of shame and indignation. That colony had absolutely no sympathy with Cromwell and his party. It was in no sense or part Puritan. The Cavalier sentiment dominated it completely; for though the bulk of its inhabitants came out very poor, and were as far as possible from being "gentlemen," they were not at all of the material of which Roundheads were made; nor had they any influence in the government of the Province. The General Assembly represented the gentlemen of the colony, who were royalists to a man.

It is not surprising, therefore, that upon the receipt of the news of the execution of Charles I, the General Assembly of Virginia lost no time in meeting and passing an act in which the dead king's son, Charles II, was recognized as the rightful and reigning sovereign. Legal processes, and the machinery of the provincial government, continued to run in the king's name. In England, Cromwell was installed as Lord Protector. But Virginia refused to recognize him or his title. At least one county of Virginia formally proclaimed Charles king, requiring "all his majesty's liege people to pray God to bless Charles the Second, King of England, Scotland, France and Ireland, Virginia, New England and the Caribda Islands." This, I believe, was the first appearance of the term "King of Virginia," a title which was destined to be heard again somewhat later.

Nor did the people content themselves with proclaiming Charles king. In 1650, Governor Berkeley sent Colonel Norwood to Holland to invite the prince to become the ruling sovereign of what Raleigh had called "the newe Inglishe Nation" on this side the water. Charles did not accept. Nor did he frankly refuse. He had not the boldness to go to Virginia, but he was delighted with the chance to put on for a moment the manner and authority of a ruler. He sent Berkeley a new commission as governor, signed by himself as king, and gave Colonel Norwood a commission as treasurer of the colony. Both commissions were honored in Virginia.

The colony, indeed, with Barbadoes in the West Indies, virtually constituted itself the Dominion of King Charles the Second; and it is in memory of that assumption of the whole kingdom's prerogative, as the Virginians believe, that the state is called the Old Dominion today.

Nor did the people propose that their allegiance should remain merely nominal. They essayed actually to cut the connection with Cromwell's Commonwealth and maintain themselves as the sovereign remainder of the English realm. They succeeded in maintaining this position for a considerable time—until, that is, 1651, when Cromwell's government sent three ships of war to reduce the Virginians to submission. As all the principal settlements were within easy reach of navigable water, and had not developed sufficient back territory by means of which to support themselves, it was impracticable for them to hold out long; they were obliged to submit. Cromwell treated the province oppressively, and forbade the other colonies to trade with it.

It is not at all surprising that Virginia, which in the meantime had become the place of refuge of many more royalists, took steps to throw off the Puritan allegiance as soon as possible after Cromwell's death, and sought to anticipate the restoration of the Stuarts. Sir William Berkeley, whom Cromwell had displaced with a Roundhead governor, was again called to the head of things by the people. He refused to assume the governorship at their mandate unless they gave him their solemn and formal promise to venture their lives and fortunes for King Charles II. This promise was given him by the unanimous voice of the electors. Berkeley then proceeded to proclaim Charles "King of England, Scotland, France, Ireland and Virginia." Virginia was once more the sole existing segment of the king's dominion. In Virginia, and in Virginia only, processes and documents were issued in his name.

Charles was therefore really king in Virginia, though in very fact he was still living a lazy and rather low life in the Dutch towns, or eating, as a guest, the bread of the French and Spanish nobility. The Virginians, however, were not at all content with having set up a mere paper sovereignty for him. Berkeley had kept in touch, by letter and through messengers, with Charles, and had sent word to him, in Holland, before the Commonwealth had fallen, that he would raise his standard in Virginia if the king would give his consent. Once more he offered him a Virginian crown. Richard Lee was sent to Holland with a proposition from Berkeley to take the field for the king. It was even proposed that Charles should come to Virginia and set up his throne there.

The king once more sent cordial thanks to the Virginians. But he did not accept their proposition. We can imagine that along one side of his nature it appealed to him, and on the other and commanding side it was quite unwelcome; that is to say, while it must have inflamed somewhat his ambition to be king once more and have done with the eating of the bread of others, it was quite in conflict with his natural indolence and moral cowardice. His first attempt to assert his kingship, when, on the field of Worcester, he was ignominiously defeated by Cromwell, had sickened him with all proceedings having the stamp of energy upon them. As a matter of fact, it would have been perfectly safe for him to raise his standard and set up his throne in Virginia. But he would not venture it. He would remain on the Continent and await the turn of events.

Ere long events made him king in England. The Commonwealth fell to pieces when there was no longer a strong hand to guide it. Charles landed shabbily, even squalidly, at Dover, almost sneaking into the country, instead of coming in triumph from Virginia, with a kingly New World in his hand, as he might have done if he had accepted Berkeley's invitation.

If, after his defeat at Worcester, he had taken advantage of Virginia's first proffer and of French assistance, and raised his flag in America, Charles might have affected the world's history very materially. There was no time when the Puritans were not in a minority in England. They held down the majority for a time because they had developed a superior military capacity, and had a splendid, resolute army. But to the nucleus of a brilliant Cavalier command in the New World, the more vigorous English royalists might have rallied. A court at Williamsburg, which was then and for a long time afterward the capital of Virginia, would have meant a royal court in London much sooner than it really arrived, and would have caused the Commonwealth to leave a fainter and narrower mark upon the history of England than in the event it did leave.

Meantime, what a brilliant court would have assembled around the gay and talkative monarch at Williamsburg! Already the Lees, the Washingtons, the Berkeleys, and many others of the "first families," were established in Virginia. Charles would probably have been happy in the easy, light-hearted atmosphere of the plantations. There were no Puritans there to bother him. Virginia had made its own laws against Puritan practices—and enforced them.

Never was a monarch who would have been better pleased with having about him actual slaves—men and women whose bodies he would have owned. His sway must have spread northward as far as the border of the French possessions, for though New England was Puritan, it bent reluctantly to the sway of the Commonwealth, seeming to scent in the Roundhead sovereignty a kind of rival that threatened to take over its half-won autonomy. A kingship exercised in America would probably have suited the men of New England very well.

In all likelihood the throne would in due time have been transferred to the mother country. But its erection here, even for a few years, must have infused into the character of the Americans generally a larger element of monarchicalism than fell to their lot as it was. Virginia would hardly have fallen off so readily into colonial republicanism as it did in

The Ifs of History

1774-1776. English neglect of a really royalist Virginia sowed the seed of Virginian rebellion. If Virginia had not supported Massachusetts, shoulder to shoulder, there could not have been an American Revolution. Charles did not know how far he let Virginia go when he rebuffed Berkeley's emissaries.

The sentiment of personal loyalty to the crown remained strong in the colonies up to the very outburst of the Revolution. The Americans dissolved the relation of subject and sovereign with regret. If they had ever had a king whom they could call their own, the interest enkindled and perpetuated by his presence might very well have turned the scale in 1776 and prevented the withdrawal of the colonies.

CHAPTER X
IF ADMIRAL PENN HAD PERSISTED IN DISOWNING HIS SON WILLIAM

When an English father, irascible and opinionated, disowns and turns out of doors a son who has not only disobeyed him but proved false to the traditions and obvious interests of the family, he is very apt to adhere to his action. A very great deal turned upon a case, once, in which an English father, after making a very firm show of disowning his son, at last relented and took him back to his heart.

Pennsylvania, to wit, turned upon it; and all the amazing success of William Penn's great experiment in colonization. There has never been anything quite like that success in the world's history, for the great trek of the already established American population in the nineteenth century was a readjustment, an extension, rather than a colonization in the true sense. The planting of Pennsylvania was a true colonization. Not only did it amount to the creation of a great and model commonwealth, full-fledged, with a composite new-world population, in twenty or even ten years' time, but it furnished the keystone to the arch of states that constituted the American republic in the next century after Penn's settlement.

Philadelphia led the American towns in the seven years of the Revolution. It was their capital commercially as well as politically. It supplied most of the sinews of war. Without

Robert Morris's $1,400,000, all of which came from Philadelphia, the final and crucial campaign of the war could not have been fought. More than that, without just the sort of commonwealth that Pennsylvania had already become, standing in the center of things—cosmopolitan, independent of royalist or aristocratic influence, populous, well-to-do, democratic, steady—it is hard to see how the Revolution could have been undertaken at all.

But for the incident which permitted Penn's settlement, the vast territory which afterward constituted Pennsylvania would have become merely an extension of New York, or of New Jersey, or of Maryland, or of Virginia, or of all of them. The chances are that its resources would have been exploited by slave labor. The greater part of the state might have remained slave territory up to 1861. In any case its development would have been much more slow, its peopling much less rapid. Not only must Indian wars have checked growth, but the spectacle of the arrival of five hundred thousand stalwart Germans, the creation of the largest city in the colonies within fifty years, and the upbuilding, in that time, of a trade from the Delaware River that employed more than five hundred ships and seven thousand sailors, could never have been presented.

The part which Pennsylvania began to play from the moment of Penn's arrival, and which it still plays, in American affairs, was directly dependent upon Penn's character and genius, and, for a long time, upon his wealth and social position. Without the wealth which William Penn inherited from his father, Admiral Sir William Penn, he could not have organized his Pennsylvania Society, nor bought the site of Philadelphia. Without the position, as well as the wealth, which he inherited, he could not, in the first place, have aspired to the acquaintance with and confidence of King Charles II; and these were absolutely essential to the extraordinary charter, in behalf of a despised and distrusted people, which Penn received at the king's hands.

Had Penn always been in this favorable position? We shall see. The admiral, his father, was a good churchman and a conservative man. King Charles held him in very high estimation. The son was brilliant, and of noble character. He was sent to Oxford University; and what was the father's astonishment, after the boy had been there some little time, to hear that he had joined the despised and persecuted sect of the Quakers! This was very much as if, at the present day, the son and heir of a great multi-millionaire should join, not merely the Socialists, but the Anarchists at Paterson!

Sir William raved and scolded. The son only grew more firm in the faith. Sir William endured much; but finding the young man actually inclined to address the king as "thou," he told him that if he committed this impropriety, or "thee-ed" and "thoued" either him, the admiral, or the Duke of York, he would disown him, and cut him off without a shilling. On the very first opportunity after this, young William addressed King Charles as "thou!" The king, having a more than royal sense of humor, made a jest of the matter, but Sir William did not. He was as good as his word. He turned his son out of doors, and bade him begone. The youth went abroad, and took up for a time a very much discredited existence. He had already been expelled from the university.

Here, for a time, the fate of Pennsylvania certainly trembled in the balance. It was quite within the outraged admiral's power to make the ban permanent. If he had done so, there would never have been a Quaker-German commonwealth in America.

It is known that the son accepted his banishment as permanent. But his mother did not. She pleaded with the father for his forgiveness. She reminded him of the boy's great natural goodness, his brilliancy, his affectionateness. He would, Lady Penn maintained, recover from his distemper of Quakerism. She begged her husband, before it was too late, to relent and recall him.

At length, moved by this appeal and the promptings of his own heart, the admiral called the young man home. Once or twice afterwards he was on the point of a more radical banishment of him. But, fortunately for the New World, Sir William's heart was soft after all. The son was reÎstablished in his good graces. After the admiral's death, in 1670, it was found that he had bequeathed all his wealth to the son, and, owing to the son's influence, the Quakers improved their position not a little, and in due time Penn organized and put through the Pennsylvania experiment. But King Charles took good care to inform him that the name "Pennsylvania," officially bestowed on the colony, was not in honor of the founder, but in compliment to the admiral, his father.

Narrow as this contingency may have been, since so great an event depended on the impulse of one man, it was after all a moral contingency, and not due of physical accident, as so many others have been. It is the more impressive for this reason. It is good to know that a few heartbeats the more, in the breast of a man who can be kind as well as hot-tempered, may create a mighty empire.

CHAPTER XI
IF GEORGE WASHINGTON HAD
BECOME A BRITISH MIDSHIPMAN

One summer day, in 1746, a British ship of war lay in the Potomac River below the place where the city of Washington now stands. The officers of the ship had been visiting at Mount Vernon, which was the residence of Major Lawrence Washington, adjutant-general of Virginia.

No vessel of the royal navy entered the Potomac River without a visit on the part of its officers to Major Washington's house. He had been in the king's service at the siege of Cartagena and elsewhere. Admiral Vernon was his friend; Major Washington's estate on the Potomac had been named after the admiral. Lawrence Washington's acquaintance with the men of both army and navy was wide, and his popularity among them great. A visit to his hospitable residence, where he entertained them with true Virginian lavishness, was always a bright spot in any naval officer's life at that day.

At Lawrence Washington's table, for two or three years prior to 1746, had sat his younger brother, George by name. This lad, who was a gentleman and a soldier in miniature, had often listened to stories of the exploits of the navy—of the capture of Porto Bello, of the bombardment of Cartagena, and of cruisings and battles along the Spanish Main. These stories and personal contact with their heroes had inspired him with an eager desire to enter the naval service. His father was dead, and his brother, who had virtually taken the father's place, favored the boy's design. His mother had opposed it. But at last she had been induced to give her consent. A midshipman's warrant was obtained for young George Washington, and on the summer day in 1746 of which we have spoken his luggage had actually been sent on board the ship lying in the river.

But at the last moment Mary Washington flatly rebelled. She could not bear the thought of her boy's going to sea. She foresaw a time when she would need him at home. She withdrew her consent; and as her signature was necessary to his enlistment, it was impossible for him to join the ship, and his luggage was sent back to Mount Vernon.

So thus it happened that George Washington did not, at the age of fourteen, enter the British navy, and embark upon a career which would probably have held him fast all the rest of his life.

It was a real contingency—that of the possible commitment of George Washington to the royal cause. Every influence that bore upon him, up to the date of his brother Lawrence's death, in 1752, was royalist. This brother was married to the daughter of George William Fairfax, cousin and manager of the great American estates of Lord Fairfax. Lord Fairfax himself, removing to Virginia, became the patron, friend and mentor of young George Washington. The young man was in constant association with Englishmen, and always more or less under official influence.

The Fairfaxes remained loyal to the British power when the war of independence was declared. If Lawrence Washington had lived it is quite conceivable—aye, probable—that he would have gone with them. If George Washington had not been thrown much into contact after that with his Virginian neighbors, among whom the spirit of rebellion had been propagated from Massachusetts—if he had not himself become a colonial soldier and commander—there can be little question that he would have clung to the English side.

In the meantime, undoubtedly, he would have been advanced to rather high rank in the naval service, if he had joined it. The years between 1746, when the midshipman's warrant was obtained for Washington, and 1774, when the colonies began to flame up into revolt, had been of great activity at sea.

The young officer might have participated in the destruction of the French fleet at Cape Finisterre; in the victory off Lagos; in the great decisive combat in Quiberon Bay; in the capture of Havana, and in many other sea fights. He would have fought by the side of Boscawen, Sir Edward Hawke, Lord Howe, Duff and Rodney, and very likely have won laurels such as theirs. Nothing colonial could have separated him from the flag which he had thus served, any more than the influence of his native state could have separated Farragut from the Stars and Stripes in 1861.

Is it too much to say that the American republic would have been fatherless without Washington? Perhaps an arm might have been found—though that is doubtful—that could have wielded his sword. But where was the brain, the patience, the tact, the determination, that would have composed the differences in the American councils, and have kept the discordant colonies and the jealous commanders together?

That another man, that any combination of men, could have done what he did, is inconceivable. In the grandeur of his character and in the genius with which he accomplished a tremendous work, he is uncompanioned not only in America, but in the history of the world. Without his steadying hand in the war, the American army would have followed a devious course to death, and the young republic one to its destruction.

As to the decisive part which he played in the formation of the union of the States after the war, the word of his companions in the Federal Constituent Convention is conclusive. "Were it not for one great character in America," said Grayson of Virginia, referring to Washington, "so many men would not be for this government; we do not fear while he lives, but who besides him can concentrate the confidence and affection of all Americans?" No one else ever could have concentrated them. Monroe reported to Jefferson, "Be assured Washington's influence carried this government." And Bancroft has put this judgment on record: "The country was an instrument with thirteen strings, and the only master who could bring out all their harmonious thought was Washington. Had the idea prevailed that he would not accept the Presidency, it would have proved fatal."

Washington was the pivot upon which all things turned. Lacking such a pivot, the machinery of the American republic would have tumbled into ruin. Happy the choice of the Virginian mother who could not spare her boy on that summer day, and sent aboard the man-of-war in Potomac's stream for his dunnage!

CHAPTER XII
IF ALEXANDER HAMILTON HAD
NOT WRITTEN ABOUT A HURRICANE

"He thought out the Constitution of the United States and the details of the government of the Union; and out of the chaos that existed after the Revolution raised a fabric every part of which is instinct with his thought." So said one of his contemporaries, Ambrose Spencer, of Alexander Hamilton; and another said: "He did the thinking of his time." The thinking that Hamilton did for the young American republic was of the most tremendous and vital importance to it. His services as a financier were not merely of a negative or saving character—they were positively constructive and permanently enduring; he "created a public credit and brought the resources of the country into active efficiency." It was Hamilton who founded the American system of business and finance.

Yet it is altogether likely that but for an accidental circumstance or two Alexander Hamilton would never have come to the continental colonies. He was born on the Island of Nevis, in the West Indies, and upon that island, and upon St. Christopher and St. Croix, neighboring islands, his life up to the age of fifteen was spent. His father, James Hamilton, had proved "feckless and unfortunate," as a British biographer of Hamilton expresses it, and early ceased to provide for the boy, or, apparently, to take any interest in his education or welfare. His mother died early, and left him to the charge of her relatives, and as she bequeathed to them several other children, they had little thought about Alexander except to make him of some use and lighten their own burden. He was sent to school scarcely at all, and at the age of twelve was put into the shop or store of Nicholas Cruger, a general dealer at St. Croix, to earn his living as a clerk.

There he remained for about three years. He has often been described as phenomenally precocious, and he certainly was, in the sense that his mind ripened early. But there was nothing of the quality of smart, self-satisfied immaturity about his genius. He read much, studied deeply, and received some good training at the hands of Rev. Hugh Knox, a Presbyterian minister.

But all at once there occurred the accident which resulted in his going to the continental colonies. In the late summer of 1772 a fearful hurricane swept over the Leeward Islands. The boy Hamilton, then fifteen years old, had his full share in the adventures attending this calamity, and wrote a long and vivid account of it for a newspaper published at St. Christopher. By this brilliant piece of news work the entire West Indies were electrified. The people there had had plenty of hurricanes before, but none of them had ever been adequately "written up." Young Hamilton awoke one morning to find himself in the enjoyment of a fame which extended all the way from Jamaica to Trinidad.

The immediate result of this notoriety was to convince Alexander's relatives that they possessed in him a prodigy, and to stimulate them to find means to educate him. They raised a fund forthwith without any particular difficulty, and shipped him, armed with a letter of introduction from Rev. Mr. Knox, to Boston, en route to New York. Lacking this assistance, it is unlikely that the youth would have found his way to our shores. Perhaps he would, in spite of everything, have risen to eminence in the West Indies. Very likely he would one day have drifted to Scotland or England, and he might have become a famous man there. But America would have lost him.

There is still another and vital contingency associated with Hamilton's removal to the American continent. On its way to Boston, while in the open ocean, the ship on which he had sailed took fire. For some time it was in danger of destruction. But with great difficulty the flames were extinguished. If they had prevailed, the career of the West Indian genius would doubtless have been cut short by death.

Thus, by the aid, first, of a tropical hurricane, and, second, through the efforts of the crew of the ship that bore him, in stifling a fire in the hold, Alexander Hamilton reached the American colonies just in time to be swept into the current of the movement for independence; to be made over anew into an ardent American, and to put his stamp forever upon the young nation which arose from the smoke of Bunker Hill. The dark-skinned, dark-eyed, exotic-looking student at King's College, whom the citizens of New York at first looked at askance as a very "queer West Indian," became a great leader, a commander, a guide, a magnificent constructive as well as restraining force.

What this country would have been without him, or rather, what it must forever have failed to be, may be inferred from the things which it became that were owed to him. He was the inventor of American protection. American industry was founded upon his "report on manufactures." As the first and greatest of Federalists, he saved the confederation from disruption by supplying the idea of central authority. Others might labor for freedom—he labored for security. He put reason at the bottom of our commonwealth. Without his principles, the republic would have lacked a balance wheel. The States' rights would have been everything—the nation's rights nothing.

All our national expansion was wrapped up in Hamilton's views. McKinley and Roosevelt have been his continuators. The sentiment which governs our republic today is Hamiltonian; and the war and discord that have afflicted us, as the result of the looseness of our confederation, must long since have wrecked the nation but for the balance wheel with which he supplied us.

CHAPTER XIII
IF LA FAYETTE HAD HELD THE
FRENCH REIGN OF TERROR IN CHECK

In every age of the world, and in every place, one voice has always commanded in the affairs of nations, peoples and communities. If oligarchies, legislatures, groups or cabals have seemed to bear sway, it has nevertheless been true that in each of these groups, from time to time, the influence of some individual has been preponderant. The freest republics are an organization of this principle—a willing submission of the many to the leadership of chosen men.

In times of stress and strife and change it is impossible that strong men should not seize the reins of power, no matter what political system exists, no matter what anarchy tends to prevail. Change, indeed, makes the opportunity of the strong; and the fate of nations and continents depends upon the character of the strong man who is brought forth. If he is good, as Washington was good, his fellow-countrymen derive lasting and unmeasured benefit from his grasping of his opportunity. If he is bad, as Napoleon Bonaparte was bad, the evil harvest of his vices may be reaped through generations and centuries, as France has reaped, and is now reaping, an inheritance of strife and national decline.

When the Revolution of 1789 came to France there were many people, of all parties and conditions, who believed that the country had its Washington. He was to be found, they thought, in the person of the Marquis de La Fayette. This man was Washington's friend. He had successfully copied many of his virtues. He was unselfishly patriotic. He believed in the liberty of the people, and wished to see them govern themselves. Though himself a nobleman, he believed in the abolition of titles of nobility. In his room, and afterward in his office as a public servant, he kept two frames hanging on the wall. In one frame was a copy of the American Declaration of Independence. The other frame was empty, but it bore the legend, "This space awaits the French Declaration of Independence."

When the Revolution broke out, La Fayette was called by the people to the center of real power—the command of the troops in Paris. Both king and people trusted him. His power for good was almost absolute. He prevented anarchy and restored order in Paris after the overthrow of the Bastille. He gave the country a Bill of Rights and a Constitution founded on the American models. The quarrels of the warring factions were stayed by his hand. The mob dared not turn the king out. La Fayette's moderating influence was the ballast that kept the French nation, in spite of certain excesses, on a steady keel.

Even when the Girondists and Jacobins rose and were ready to fly at one another's throats, the fear of La Fayette kept these factions from violence. If he had maintained this influence—if he had preserved the sagacity and boldness to side with the people and lead them—the French nation might have been saved from anarchy, reaction, the tyrannies of emperors and of mobs, and the slow degeneration that has followed its long diet of gunpowder.

But in the test La Fayette did not exhibit this power. In 1792 he was in the field, in command of an army, resisting the Prussian invasion. The nation, aroused, was equal to the task of repelling foreign attack. But in Paris events were marching. The people rose and overthrew the throne and the royalist Constitution which La Fayette had made. But they turned still to La Fayette. They offered him the chief executive power in the new government.

This was his opportunity to save France. He was not equal to it. He did not rise to the emergency. He not only refused the offer of power, but made his troops renew their oaths of fidelity to the king. Then the Assembly declared him a traitor; and La Fayette, taking with him a few followers, deserted his command, made his way to Bouillon, on the frontier, and rode out of France into a foreign land!

No man can imagine Washington taking such a step as that. La Fayette suffered from it, and he afterwards served his country nobly. But the eternal mischief of his weakness had been done. Girondists and Jacobins, relieved from the fear of him, turned to mutual destruction and murder. The Reign of Terror was on. The nation was plunged in an orgy of blood. Four hundred thousand men and women were put to death. Liberty in France was assassinated in the house of its friends.

One man, I have said, always comes to the top of things. With La Fayette gone, Robespierre, the man of blood, prevailed. Robespierre was the Terror. And after him, the Terror having appeased its fearful thirst, and Robespierre's head having gone into the basket with his victims', there came another man to take advantage of the paralysis the perverted Revolution had inflicted upon France. That man was Napoleon Bonaparte.

Bonaparte freed La Fayette from captivity. Bonaparte held him in contempt, calling him a "noodle." It was not so bad as that. But Napoleon despised a man who had had his chance and failed to grasp it.

Had La Fayette proved equal to that opportunity, France would have been organized as a constitutional republic. The Terror would not have been. Napoleon's ambition might have been held in check. The balance in Europe would have been maintained, but the leadership of France would have been consolidated and become immortal. The nations would have followed her example. Monarchy would have died of dry rot. The dream of a United States of Europe might have been realized—perhaps with a city of La Fayette, the capital of the vast confederation, the European equivalent city of Washington, smiling down, it may be, from the neutral shores of the Lake of Constance to east, to west, to north, to south, with a benediction of peace.

CHAPTER XIII
IF GILBERT LIVINGSTON HAD NOT
VOTED NEW YORK INTO THE UNION

How many Americans of the present day realize that the State of New York, at the time of the adoption of the national Constitution, was radically and overwhelmingly opposed to entrance into the Union which the Constitution proposed, and was at last forced into the league of States only by the demonstration that the State would be isolated and cut off from its neighbor States if it did not join, with a tariff wall raised against it? It is indeed hard for New Yorkers to realize, as they live today under the Stars and Stripes, having forgotten what their State flag is, and being among the most zealous supporters of the Union, that their State led the opposition to the Constitution, and that but for the influence of a very few men in two other States, New York might have prevented the consummation of that "more perfect union."

The contingency that prevented the State from dismembering the Union at its start was a narrow one, but it had been provided for. Hamilton and the Federalists had laid their plans well. They first furnished the Southern States, and the smallest States in the North, with an interested reason for joining the Union. They gave the men of the South representation on their slaves. They made the little States equal with the great States in the Senate. Then they provided that when nine States had ratified the Constitution it should become effective, and a confederation should be formed by those nine States, if there were no others.

Then the ratifications began. The game was to get nine States. Little Delaware said "Yes" first. Franklin and Wilson had a firm hold upon Pennsylvania, and that State entered next under the pressure they exerted. New Jersey, Georgia, Connecticut, Massachusetts, Maryland and South Carolina followed. This made eight States. Then things stuck fast. Would there be a ninth?

Two thirds of the delegates in the convention of New York were firmly opposed to ratification. They believed the Constitution meant an end of the liberties of the States. They saw a royal throne looming up for America. They feared, they said, a great central power which should oppress and overtax the people of the States. Governor Clinton led the opposition to ratification. Hamilton's able arguments had no effect. New York would not come in.

All the remaining States were believed to be also opposed. New Hampshire had refused to comply with the requisitions of the Confederation; why should it look with more favor on the Constitution? In Virginia, Patrick Henry led the opposition to ratification with impassioned eloquence. Richard Henry Lee, William Grayson, George Mason and James Monroe, all great men in the State, were unalterably opposed to ratification. It certainly looked black for the Union.

But in this moment of apparent triumph, while the New York convention was in session, Governor Clinton and his party in the convention heard surprising news. New Hampshire, under the influence of Massachusetts and of the wiser counsels of some of its own leaders, ratified the Constitution on the 21st of June, 1788—more than nine months after the adoption of the instrument by the Constitutional Convention at Philadelphia.

This event put a new face on the situation in New York. The Union was now decreed. If New York did not enter it, she must be prepared to stand alone, as an independent nation. Could she do that? The new Confederation would hem her in on both sides. To it would belong New Jersey, which flanked her only seaport on the west, and Connecticut and Massachusetts, which walled her in on the east. The shape of the State adapted it very badly indeed for an independent position. Moreover, influences were known to be at work which would precipitate a hostile tariff against the States which remained out of the Union. A few months later such a tariff was actually adopted against Rhode Island, which was treated as a foreign country in the levying of duties on imports.

New York could not stand that. Gilbert Livingston and a few others changed their votes under a distinct announcement that the pressure of "sister States" had made it impracticable to continue the opposition. But even at the last, the Constitution was ratified by a majority of only two in a vote of sixty! Gilbert Livingston held the fate of the State in his hands, and he, though pledged against the Union, put New York into the Union by his vote.

One vote would have kept New York out.

We have noted the fact that New York's position was unfavorable for an attempt at independence. But the fact that the voice of but one man prevented the attempt shows that the other opposing delegates were not much afraid of making the leap. Supposing Gilbert Livingston had voted the other way, and the vote had been thirty-one to twenty-nine against ratification, instead of the same figure in its favor? What would have resulted?

Let us see. Two other States were radically opposed to the Constitution—Rhode Island and North Carolina. Very likely they would have been glad to form a defensive alliance with New York. Virginia ratified a few days after New Hampshire, but she might easily have retracted her ratification, for she had no heart in it. With Virginia, the malcontent States would have had (census of 1790) a population of 1,550,306, against 2,378,908 for the remaining colonies, including

Vermont, which was not yet in. This would not have been an utterly hopeless foundation for a new league, constituted on the easy terms upon which, and upon which only, these States were willing to enter the Union. The want of contiguity of territory would have been the worst objection to the formation of the league.

But the real effect of New York's self-exclusion, so narrowly prevented, would have been a negative one. It would have prevented all cohesion in the new Union. It would have driven a wedge straight through the new republic, from west to east. Worse, it would have erected secession into a principle from the start. Ere long we should have had at least three republics instead of one, and probably more. Politically we should have been what Central and South America are now. Real progress would have been barred. Wars would have been probable between the States. European political influences would have penetrated the weaker States, or alliances of States.

In short, the "American idea," government of the people by the people and for the people, would probably have been stillborn. By his change of vote, Gilbert Livingston signed the death warrant of the principle of secession. Not only did he set going the unifying influences which prevailed over State sovereignty, but he decreed the Empire State, destined to be a bulwark against disunion.

CHAPTER XV
IF THE PIRATE JEAN LAFITTE HAD
JOINED THE BRITISH AT NEW ORLEANS

After the battle of New Orleans, on the 8th of January, 1814, General Andrew Jackson, the victorious commander, called before him a certain officer, of dashing and Frenchy appearance, and publicly thanked him for the important part which he had borne in the battle. To judge from the signal honor done to this man, the credit for the victory was in no inconsiderable part due to him. And, indeed, this was the case.

The man to whom the victor's thanks had been thus conspicuously awarded was Jean Lafitte, the Baratarian pirate. That the success of Jackson in defeating and virtually destroying the army of Pakenham, consisting of the very flower of the Duke of Wellington's soldiery, hinged, in an important sense, upon this extraordinary corsair and buccaneer, has never been adequately acknowledged in American history.

Jean Lafitte, the foremost of the three pirate brothers of Barataria, was a man of extraordinary influence and popularity among the French and other Latin inhabitants of Louisiana and New Orleans. He was a native of France, and a brave and chivalrous corsair, as corsairs go. A price had already been put upon his head by the American governor, Claiborne. But so secure was Lafitte in the affections of the Creole people, whom he served in many ways, that he frequently attended parties and receptions in New Orleans. Arriving, on such occasions, in the full splendor of his outlaw state, and bringing joy to the heart of every lady in the room by his attractive manners as well as by his fame, the pirate chief would practically defy the authorities to lay a hand upon him. If agents of the law were sent to arrest him, he knew of it, through a hundred spies, long before they reached the place, and withdrew at once to some near-by hiding place which was well known to him. In New Orleans he had a hundred safe places of refuge.

Under his command was a force of pirates who were many or few, according to the exigencies of the moment; for they could masquerade as peaceful fishermen if necessary, or they could, upon occasion, muster a force of several hundred at a word's notice—always perfectly armed, perfectly drilled, thoroughly redoubtable.

Lafitte preyed impartially upon all the commerce of the Gulf of Mexico, and, when pursued, ran into one of the numerous mouths of the Mississippi or some inlet of the Gulf— into Barataria Lake, into Bayou Lafourche, or into Bayou Teche. There it was vain to follow him, for the intricacies of these passages were known only to his men or to the dwellers along their shores, who were in sympathy with him.

When the British descended upon New Orleans in the autumn of 1813, they offered Jean Lafitte a captain's commission in the British naval service, thirty thousand dollars in money, a full pardon for past offenses and rewards in money and lands for his followers if he would join them in making war on the Americans. He could easily have done so. The French people of Louisiana had no keen loyalty for the Stars and Stripes at that time. As Lafitte went they might have gone. The British knew this, and made their bait a rich one.

But Lafitte, although Claiborne's price was on his head, and his brother Pierre in prison in New Orleans, refused the offer. Instead, he sent the letters from Captain Lockyer, of the British navy, making this proposition, to the Louisiana legislature. Later, after Pierre had escaped, he actually joined General Jackson's nondescript army with a force of riflemen. He seems to have acted from a very honest love for the young American republic.

Jackson, at first, under a misapprehension of the circumstances, had refused to accept the aid of these "hellish banditti," as he had called Lafitte's men in a proclamation on his arrival. But when he found that the British were upon him, and that a considerable proportion of his poorly equipped militia were without flints for their muskets, he not only accepted the flints that Lafitte sent him, but gave the pirate an important command on his right wing. There Jean and his men performed signal service.

If Lafitte had joined the British with his men and ships, there is little likelihood that the Americans would have had in this fight the powerful aid of the vessels of war *Carolina* and *Louisiana*, on the river. Nor is it likely that they would have had the passive support of the French population. Nor that they would have found any substitute for the flints with which Lafitte supplied them. And it is very likely that the British assault upon Jackson's entrenchments would have been attended with a different result.

Jackson, indeed, might have been crushed very much as Windsor had been crushed at Washington, not long before.

Such a result at New Orleans would not have affected the outcome of the war, for a peace favorable to the American arms had already been declared at Ghent. But how profoundly a defeat would have influenced the personal and political fortunes of Andrew Jackson and all the events in American history which hung upon his subsequent career!

General Jackson won the presidency in 1828 because he was the military hero of the day. His popularity was due to the brilliant victory that he won at New Orleans. After his defeat in 1824, a spectacular visit which he made to the field of the 1814 battle renewed the souvenirs of the great fight and intensified his popularity; and in 1828 he was triumphantly elected. If he had been defeated in battle by Pakenham, and New Orleans had been taken, his fame would have been extinguished then and there.

And without Jackson—should we ever have had machine politics? It was he who introduced these into our government. He was the inventor and discoverer of the spoils system. "To the victors belong the spoils" was the maxim of his lieutenant, Marcy, and his own principle of action. We have never been able quite to shake off the system which he fastened upon the country. Patronage has been the curse of our politics from that day to this.

Then there was his determined and disastrous assault on the United States Bank. Upon this institution, which was founded by Alexander Hamilton, and whose position somewhat resembled the present position of the Bank of England, the financial system of the country depended. Jackson attacked it as a "wicked monopoly," as a concrete expression of the "money power." He succeeded in wrecking the bank, in bringing on the panic of 1837, which wrought untold ruin and disaster to the people, and in inaugurating in its place the system of wildcat State banks and currency chaos which lasted up to the Civil War.

But Jackson attacked more than the United States Bank and the principle that public office is a public trust. He attacked nullification. Nullification meant that the States could refuse to recognize or obey the laws of the United States. He struck that dictum hard, when it made its appearance in South Carolina, and paralyzed it to such an extent that the portion of the nation which did not believe in secession was able to get its preponderant growth, and organize its strength, and prevent disunion, when the test finally came.

Jackson saved the Union by stunning the nullification snake until the republic was big enough and strong enough to trample it under foot. And that, no doubt, was the greatest event that hung on the contingency of Lafitte's choice of sides at New Orleans.

CHAPTER XVI
IF JAMES MACDONNEL HAD NOT CLOSED
THE GATES OF HUGOMONT CASTLE

According to the Duke of Wellington himself, the success of the allies at the Battle of Waterloo turned on an amazingly slight contingency, namely, the closing of a gate or door of wood in the wall of a building. This fact was conclusively brought out when, years after the battle, an English clergyman, Rev. Mr. Narcross of Framlingham, died and left in his will the sum of five hundred pounds simply "to the bravest man in England." The executors of the estate were completely nonplussed. Who was the bravest man in England? Doubtless many would have come forward gladly to claim the distinction and the legacy, but who was worthy of them? In their trouble, the executors applied to the Duke of Wellington for an answer to the question.

The Iron Duke was not a man to be beaten by any question whatsoever, least of all by a military one. He went back a little in his recollections—until he came to the battle of Waterloo. Then he wrote to the executors of the Framlingham parson that that battle was the greatest that had been fought in recent times. "The success of it," he went on to say, "turned upon the closing of the gates of Hugomont; these gates were closed in the most courageous manner, at the very nick of time, by Sir James Macdonnel; and he is the man to whom you should pay the five hundred pounds."

Thereupon the executors went to Sir James with the money; but he said to them: "I cannot claim all the credit of closing the gates of Hugomont. My sergeant, John Graham, seeing with me the importance of the step, rushed forward to help me; and by your leave I will share the legacy with him." The request was granted, and the fact was to this extent judicially established that Sir James Macdonnel and John Graham had closed the gates of Hugomont Castle, thereby settling the issue of the battle and the fate of Europe.

Let us see what events hinged upon this act, and how they depended on it. The army with which the great Napoleon faced the miscellaneous assortment of British, Prussians, Hanoverians, Dutch and Belgians at Waterloo was smaller than that of the Allies, but vastly more efficient as a whole. Most of the troops of the Allies were raw, and some of them were poor stuff indeed. Napoleon's soldiers were hardened, practiced, brave and splendidly commanded.

Napoleon had forced the Allies back at Quatre Bras. He captured their position at La Haye Sainte. He perceived that the strategic key to the whole field of battle was the hill crowned by the old stone *château* of Hugomont. If that could be taken, Napoleon would be able to attack and turn Wellington's right flank. That accomplished, a junction of Blücher and his Prussians with the English would be prevented; the forces of the Allies would be split in two, and Napoleon would in all probability defeat them in detail, according to his time-honored method. The emperor could easily have finished off the Austrians in their turn, as he planned to do; and the combined European attempt to oust him would have been frustrated. Thus the Corsican would have been, probably for so long as he lived, the master of France at the least, even if the checks he had already received had restricted his mastery of the rest of the continent.

Knowing well that upon this cast his fate was staked, Napoleon hurled his best troops, under Prince Jerome, against the little old *château* on the hill. Again and again they assaulted it. Twelve thousand men were launched against the half-dilapidated castle, which had been pierced with loopholes for the British riflemen. And now and here came the crucial incident whose importance was rated so high by Wellington. At a moment when the chief defence of the *château* was entrusted to the Coldstream Guards, under Colonel James Macdonnel, the French were within a hair's breadth of taking it. They pushed against the gate of the castle, and had actually forced it open, when the Coldstream Guards charged out with their bayonets, forcing the advance rank of the French back a little.

But the French were pouring up, and could no longer be held back at the point of the bayonet. It was at this instant, when a slight leeway had been gained, that Colonel Macdonnel and Sergeant Graham, under a galling fire from the French, stepped forward and with their own hands closed the *château* gates, barricaded them, and thus enabled the troops to resume their fierce rifle fire from within.

After this the French made many more assaults on the heavy gates, but could not force them open again. Wellington meanwhile commanded a general advance, following a fresh repulse of the French onset; and the French line was thrown into confusion. He knew that Blücher was now at hand—it was by this time half-past seven in the evening—to support him. Blücher, indeed, arrived, and attacked and crushed the broken French right, forcing Napoleon to retreat in disorder. Thus was completed the victory which the heroic defence of Hugomont had made possible.

The crushing of the British right wing on this occasion, had Napoleon been able thus to effect it, would have reversed a vast deal of history. It is not necessary to take an extreme view of the situation to realize this. On the immediate field, the British, Dutch and Hanoverians must have been forced back upon Brussels, and Blücher would have been unable to maintain a front against the French. Even if the remnants of the allied armies had escaped, and made another stand, Napoleon must instantly have regained a degree of prestige and position that would have enabled him to consolidate his power at home and make excellent terms abroad. Even after Leipsic, when he had seemed to be utterly beaten, the powers had been willing to give him France's "natural frontiers"—namely, the Rhine, the Alps and the Pyrenees.

It is likely that Leipsic and Elba had already taught the emperor wisdom which would have deterred him from attempting to carry the boundaries of his domain once more to the Baltic, or to parcel out the rest of Europe among his relatives and dependents. But within the frontiers I have named, and west of the Rhine, he must have remained impregnable; and all the momentous consequences which resulted from his defeat must have been thwarted and turned aside.

Out of the victory of the Allies at Waterloo came, first, the banishment and early death of Napoleon Bonaparte; the placing of Louis XVIII on the throne of France; the complete subduing of the Revolution; the creation of the joint kingdom of Holland and Belgium (which meant the modern intensely industrialized Belgian state, and Leopold, and the Congo); the aggrandizement and lasting leadership of Prussia in Germany; the foundation of the modern Italy through the annexation of the Genoese republic to the Piedmont kingdom; the enlargement of Switzerland by three cantons taken from France; the taking of Norway from Denmark and its bestowal upon Sweden; the absorption of what was left of Poland by Russia—and some other reparceling of territory in an arbitrary sense which has nevertheless for the most part endured. There is scarcely a political articulation in Europe today which does not date from Waterloo; new tendencies still operate which had their inception then!

Indirectly the consequences were momentous. The aggrandizement of Prussia prepared the way for the unification of Germany and the gradual atrophy of Austria as a German state. As I have said, the enlargement of Piedmont foretokened a united Italy, and built up another power which has contributed to the enforced shrinkage of Austria. The two great constructive European statesmen of the nineteenth century, Bismarck and Cavour, were both the children of Waterloo.

All these tendencies might have been working just the other way if Colonel Macdonnel had not succeeded in closing the *château* gates! Yet more still was in store. Moral and intellectual consequences of greater moment, perhaps, than the political results, impended. The victory of the Allies was followed by a period of severe repression of popular tendencies in Europe. The Holy Alliance, which became a league of Continental monarchs against liberal ideas, was a direct consequence. It inaugurated reaction everywhere. And reaction bred in its turn new and insidious radicalisms. Lassalle, Marx, St. Simon, and Fourier, Socialists, and Bakunin and Proudhon, first of the Anarchists, were the offspring of the Holy Alliance, nurtured in the dark corners of Repression's jail.

The course of events in Europe would have been far otherwise indeed if Napoleon's veterans, forcing their way into Hugomont and splitting the British strength in two, had prepared the way for a long lease of the power of that adroit and calculating master, who knew so well how to meet popular demands and still hold his personal sway. In its practical expression, his system was liberal. Every peasant proprietor in France today holds his acres by virtue of Napoleonic legislation.

That does not mean that all would have been good in France; far from that. A strange falsity, a theatric insincerity, lay beneath all the Napoleonic sentiments and ideals. These qualities color the thought of France still. Will she ever be able to escape them? These tendencies would have been many times more powerful if Napoleon had entrenched himself upon the throne. More than that, they must have passed to other countries. The shadow of his eagles might lie athwart even our America, his insidious ideas expressing themselves in our politics and our intellectual and moral life,

The Ifs of History

if that moment's vast contingency had gone Napoleon's way at Waterloo.

CHAPTER XVII
IF ABRAHAM LINCOLN'S FATHER HAD
MOVED SOUTHWARD, NOT NORTHWARD

The two sections in the Civil War in America were led by two men, Abraham Lincoln and Jefferson Davis, the one President of the United States and the other President of the Confederate States, who were born within about one hundred miles of each other in the State of Kentucky, and within nine months of each other in point of time. For it was in June, 1808, that Jefferson Davis first saw the light in Christian County, Kentucky, and in February, 1809, that Abraham Lincoln was born in Hardin County, in the same State.

Samuel Davis, the father of Jefferson Davis, and Thomas Lincoln, the father of Abraham Lincoln, were men of the same English-American origin, and the families were originally of virtually the same class, though Thomas Lincoln, doubtless as the result of the death of his father at the hands of the Indians, when Thomas was a child, had fallen somewhat in the social scale. Both men became dissatisfied with material conditions in Kentucky at about the same time, and both emigrated with their families. But Samuel Davis went southward into Mississippi, while Thomas Lincoln went northward into Indiana.

That the sons of both these Kentuckians had in them the fire of genius, the history of their country has abundantly proved. Each was destined by the compelling force of his character and gifts to play a great part. Like all other men, each was molded by his environment. The illiterate Thomas Lincoln was credited by his immortal son with the intention, in emigrating, to escape from a slave State. But is it not probable that the son, deeply preoccupied as he was in later years with the subject of the emancipation of the slaves, had projected backward, by a psychologic habit common to all mankind, this idea from his own mind into that of his father? In all probability no other motive than that of accident or convenience—for Thomas Lincoln was a poor and rather "shiftless" man—impelled Abraham Lincoln's father to go to Indiana instead of following the trail which so many of the more enterprising Kentuckians were taking to Mississippi or Louisiana. It was to that section that enterprise beckoned, for agriculture was carried on in the Southwest upon a large scale, and broader plantations were open to the adventuring settler. Indiana, on the other hand, was a "poor man's country."

What if Thomas Lincoln had possessed a little more energy, and a few more shillings, and had gone to Mississippi instead of to Indiana and afterwards to Illinois? What if he had become a plantation and slave owner, and had thus subjected his boy Abraham to the overmastering influence of a southern environment? So far as I can recall, Mississippi never produced an anti-slavery man.

In this event, there would have been for the national cause, for the saving of the Union, for the emancipation of the slaves, no Abraham Lincoln. On the other hand, the tremendous power and patience of Lincoln's nature, the majesty and greatness of his character, the resources of his intellect, would in all likelihood have been added to the sum of the statesmanship which was enlisted on the Southern side.

It is even conceivable that Lincoln, rather than Davis, would have been the president of the Southern Confederacy.

Only a combination of the most extraordinary circumstances made him the nominee of the Republican party for the presidency in 1860. If he had been the leading statesman and politician of Mississippi, his path to the Confederate presidency, as the success of Davis proved, would have been comparatively easy.

Without Lincoln, the anti-slavery agitation would have gone on just the same. The Republican party would have been constituted just the same. Everything up to the 18th day of May, 1860, when Lincoln was nominated for president at the Wigwam in Chicago, would have gone on just the same. But lacking Lincoln, what a world of things afterward would have happened differently!

In the first place, it is probable that Seward would have been nominated for president. Very likely he would not have been elected; and as it was Lincoln who "smoked out" Douglas, it is probable that Douglas would have prevailed over all other Democratic candidates and been nominated at Charleston and elected president.

In which case there would have been no secession, and very likely no war, either at that time or later. Slavery would have become intrenched, to yield, perhaps, in the end only to economic influences, the operation of which had already doomed it.

But if Seward had been nominated and elected, secession would have taken place and war would have resulted. The sort of leader that the Union would have had in Seward may be inferred with perfect certainty from the famous, or rather infamous, proposition entitled, "Some Thoughts for the President's Consideration," which Seward solemnly laid before Lincoln less than a month after his inauguration. This extraordinary document, one of the most senseless and wicked programmes ever prepared by a man of state, advocated a change of the national issue from slavery to a foreign war; it advised that war be at once declared against France and Spain, and "explanations demanded" from Great Britain and Russia! In order that this brilliant programme might be carried out successfully, Seward suggested that he himself be made Dictator!

This scheme, I repeat, illustrated the sort of alternative material that we should have had, lacking Lincoln. Chase, indeed, who was also a leading candidate for the presidency, would have been wiser. But in no position that he ever held, after 1860, did Chase bring forth any of the fruits of genius. Cameron, of Pennsylvania, was a greater man, but did not command general support. Neither did Edward Bates, of Missouri, also a western candidate for the presidency.

The great soldiers who finally triumphed in the field as the instruments of Lincoln's policy and fought their way to victory for the Union—Grant, Sherman, Thomas, Meade, Sheridan—would have been ranged on the Northern side just the same whether Lincoln or another had been at the head of affairs. But it is doubtful whether another president would have found them out. Lincoln made his own grave mistakes regarding men. But he put forward no general because that general was *his man*. He observed and waited. A man of the people himself, grandly simple, he somehow nosed out the men of the same type. All the generals who proved great were his discoveries.

The structure of Lincoln's achievements was not, however, the result of negative circumstances. It did not rise because things were not just so and so. It was a positive thing—the result of the active operations of a powerful genius, which the people recognized before the politicians and the writers did. In the people's mind, the war was "Old Abe's" war. It was Old Abe who stood at the helm. Congress did not know it, but it was really working Lincoln's will. The cabinet did not always know it, but it was Lincoln who really had his way. He kept his own counsel. He carried out his plans.

The people were right. It was Old Abe who was doing things. And without him the most important things would have gone undone. He was an original creation—as Lowell said, a "new birth of our new soil, the first American." Nature, for him, threw aside her old-world molds,

Chamberlin

And, choosing sweet clay from the breast
Of the unexhausted West,
With stuff untainted shaped a hero new,
Wise, steadfast in the strength of God, and true.

Yet what could be clearer than that Abraham Lincoln, who by birth and inheritance was of the South, not the West, might have turned his strength to the support of quite a different cause if the accident of fate had sent him southward, not northward, in his childhood?

CHAPTER XVIII
IF SKIPPER JENNINGS HAD NOT RESCUED CERTAIN SHIPWRECKED JAPANESE

Toward the end of the year 1850, Captain Jennings, of the American bark *Auckland*, trading in Asiatic waters, picked up the shipwrecked crew of a Japanese fishing vessel, somewhere off the coast of Japan. The captain was then bound for the new port of San Francisco, which the California gold-diggings had already made an important city. He continued on his course, and in due time—that is to say, very early in the year 1851—landed at San Francisco with his party of refugees.

Here the bright little Orientals were more than a nine days' wonder. Few Americans had ever before seen a Japanese. That country was at the time more a "hermit nation" than Korea herself. Whalers and other sailors who had been wrecked on the Japanese coast had been put to cruel deaths. No white men except the Dutch had been permitted to trade with any of the Japanese cities, and the Dutch trade had fallen into decay. Japan seemed as far from our lives as is the planet Mars.

But the Japanese whom Captain Jennings had humanely rescued were kindly treated by him, and on the homeward voyage they had endeared themselves to him and his crew. He landed them at San Francisco with very favorable reports of their character, conduct and intelligence. The free-handed miners of that town wanted nothing better than somebody or something to lionize. So for a considerable time the ship-wrecked Japanese had the best of everything in San Francisco, until an opportunity arose to send them, fat and happy, back to their own country.

A full account of the incident and of the refugees was published in one of the San Francisco papers. It fell into the hands of just one man who was capable of perceiving the momentous possibilities that lay in the occurrence. This man was a commodore in the United States navy; and his name was not Perry, as the reader may at first surmise, but John H. Aulick. He was a Virginian, then in his sixty-second year; he had had a long and very honorable service, and was keen and statesmanlike in his ideas.

What Commodore Aulick saw in the incident was this: The kind and friendly reception of the Japanese waifs in America, contrasted with the ordinary treatment of white refugees in Japan, might be taken advantage of to open friendly relations with Japan. To effect this result, a naval expedition should be sent to Japan. If properly conducted, the expedition not only might secure friendly treatment of American whalers on the Japanese coasts, but might open up trade relations with the country which would be highly profitable.

Filled with his idea, which was really a great one, Commodore Aulick obtained permission to lay it before the secretary of state, who was none other than Daniel Webster. He had an interview with Mr. Webster at Washington on the 9th day of May, 1851.

Webster saw the point at once. At his instance, President Fillmore ordered the navy department to prepare a small expedition for the voyage to Japan; and when the ships were ready—they were headed by the sloop of war *Mississippi*—Commodore Aulick was put in command. He actually sailed on the voyage; but he was entrusted with the task of taking the Brazilian minister as far as Rio Janeiro on the way, and some trouble having arisen with this functionary for which Commodore Aulick was blamed, he was superseded in command of the expedition by Commodore Matthew Calbraith Perry, in command of the *Hartford.*

It was Perry, therefore, who "opened up Japan." His name will be associated, as long as the story of the two nations is told, with the event. But it was Aulick's idea, not Perry's; and it all hung upon the luck which those Japanese fishermen, waifs upon a boundless ocean, had in being picked up by a generous Yankee skipper, and in finding their way to so wholehearted and so hospitable a city toward "Mongolian" wanderers as San Francisco was—then!

If this incident had not suggested and been followed by the Aulick-Perry expedition, what then? Russian authorities have claimed that Russia was preparing a similar expedition at the time when Secretary Webster—"too zealous," according to their view—sent the United States ships on their way. There is good reason to believe that the Russian government would have been slow in making such an infinitely clever move as the Perry expedition constituted. Yet if the United States had not taken the step, Russia would have stood next in the line of logical inheritance to the idea. And if Japan had been opened under Russian auspices, its doors, instead of standing open toward the East, and consequently toward *our* West, would have opened toward the Asiatic continental West, which would have meant toward St. Petersburg.

If the Japanese had, under Russian initiative, adopted the material adjuncts of western civilization, as they finally did under ours, that civilization would have taken on a distinctly Muscovite color. The Japanese would never, indeed, have been able, under such auspices, to organize an effective resistance to Russian arms, for long before they had acquired the requisite training they must have been held firmly in the grip of the Russian military system.

The Ifs of History

That is to say, Japan would have been, step by step, annexed to the Russian empire. The Russo-Japanese war would never have been, since there would have been neither hope nor occasion for it. Most of the rich fruits of Japanese art and industry would have drifted toward Russia. The Russian empire would have been enormously enriched by the Japanese trade, and the importance of that empire immensely magnified in the history of our epoch. A reflex orientalizing influence would have rolled over Russia itself, and the course of Russian internal development altered in a degree now almost incalculable.

If Russia had not been reasonably prompt to take the step, the eyes of British statesmen must sooner or later have been opened to the opportunity. The method by which British intervention proceeds in Asiatic countries is well known. It has always had but slight regard for native sovereignty, no matter how high the state of social or artistic or intellectual development on the part of the native races affected. British administrators, or, if Japan had retained its nominal sovereignty, British "residents" or agents, would really have governed the country through the Tycoon or the Mikado, or both—preferably the Tycoon, for he was a military ruler, and affairs could have been handled more readily through him.

Events in Japan must have anticipated the subsequent history of Egypt, on a much more magnificent scale. Again, though there would have been a readier entrance for American and European trade than in the case of Russian intervention, the best of everything Japanese would certainly have gone to England. And once again, the free, independent, powerful, masterful Japanese empire of the present day, thrilling with a new life in which all the civilization of the Occident is made the handmaid of an ancient and undaunted Asiatic people, would not have been.

In the unlikely event that the Japanese, in default of Perry's expedition, had been left quite alone for another generation or two, their case would not have been better in the long run. They would simply have missed the chance they got. Left a "hermit nation," they would sooner or later have fallen under the influence of one Western country or another, and been so seriously retarded in the race of civilization that they could never have caught up.

America was the only country that could have opened to them the wonderful career that they have had. The high noon of the nineteenth century was the golden moment for the commencement of their development along the line of Western civilization. If the hour had not struck then for them it would not have struck at all. Time, the helping hand, the protecting influence of an unselfish friend among the nations, and the golden gift of destiny, were all represented for Japan in the rescuing sails of Skipper Jennings's bark, that lucky day in the wide Pacific.

CHAPTER XIX
IF ORSINI'S BOMB HAD NOT FAILED
TO DESTROY NAPOLEON III

Edward A. Freeman wrote, after the fall of the second Bonaparte empire: "The work of Richelieu is utterly undone, the work of Henry II and Louis XIV is partially undone; the Rhine now neither crosses nor waters a single rood of French ground. As it was in the first beginnings of northern European history, so it is now; Germany lies on both sides of the German river." This was not by any means the whole of the work wrought by that adventurer on an imperial throne, Napoleon III, through his disastrous war against a united Germany. He accomplished also the slaughter of five hundred thousand men, and the impoverishment of millions. He sounded the death knell of monarchical adventuring in France, which was indeed one good result of the Napoleonic debacle, but he also fastened militarism, in the form of excessive and progressively increasing peace armaments, upon Europe, and magnified public debts and taxation to the limit of endurance.

Every event here mentioned was a direct development, not of Napoleon III's original seizure of the French throne, but of the final years, and the eventual overthrow of his power—the overthrow itself due to the Franco-Prussian war. A single event, criminal in its character, might have prevented these results. That great benefits sometimes eventuate from men's crimes is no news, and no longer a marvel, to the philosopher, who, when good comes of evil, is apt to repeat the words, "God moves in a mysterious way his wonders to perform."

The evil deed to which I have here referred, which would have saved the lives of five hundred thousand people and left the river Rhine still washing the confines of France, was the aiming of Orsini's bomb on the evening of the 14th of January, 1858. This bomb was designed to take the life of the emperor of the French. If the attempt had succeeded, and Napoleon had died as Alexander II of Russia and King Humbert of Italy afterward died, there would have been no Franco-German war. The throne of the baby Napoleon IV, who was then less than two years old, very likely would not have endured long; but whether the third republic had immediately arisen, or whether the Orleans Bourbons had been restored to the throne, it would have been found easy to preserve the peace with Prussia and Germany.

For Napoleon III deliberately, and with malignant ingenuity, provoked war with Germany in 1870. There is now no doubt that Bismarck desired such a war. He afterward confessed that he deceived the aged King William in such a way that all chance of peace at Ems was lost. But nevertheless the provocation of Napoleon was direct and deliberate.

His grievance was that the Hohenzollern prince, Leopold, had consented to become a candidate for the vacant throne of Spain. King William withdrew Prince Leopold's candidature. This really destroyed Napoleon's pretext for bringing on a war. But he desired a foreign war in order to forestall revolutionary opposition at home, which threatened to become irresistible. Napoleon thereupon caused his ambassador, Benedetti, insolently, and in a manner quite unbearable, to demand personally from King William a declaration that no Hohenzollern should ever be permitted to become king of

Spain. King William treated this insolence as it deserved, and France, thereupon, declared war against Prussia.

What followed, the world knows. The consequences were tremendous. France was maimed of Alsace and Lorraine. Half a million of the flower of the manhood of both nations perished. France taxed herself with five millions of francs of indemnity, and though she has paid the debt to Germany, she still owes it to her own citizens. The difficulties of French government and finance were increased prodigiously and indefinitely by the war and the empire's delinquencies.

And all as a result contingent upon the failure of a criminal act! Felice Orsini meant to kill Napoleon III, and he and his two companions did kill ten innocent persons, and did wound one hundred and fifty others. Yet the man for whom their bombs were intended—the adventurer who had once been their comrade as a member of the Italian secret society, the Carbonari, but who had afterward betrayed the cause of Italian independence by leading an army into the peninsula and restoring the papal power—escaped unharmed, to wind the trail of his infamous conspiracies through European politics for twelve years longer. If the bomb had done its direful work, one man, utterly without character or conscience, would have died, and five hundred thousand men, mostly honest, good and true, would have lived. As it happened, the one man was spared, to make a vast holocaust of human life twelve years later.

It is, indeed, strange that the averting of a single crime may sometimes precipitate a myriad of other crimes.

CHAPTER XX
IF PRESIDENT BUCHANAN HAD
ENFORCED THE LAW IN NOVEMBER, 1860

Speaking of the lighting of the fires of civil war in this country in the years 1860 and 1861, Charles Francis Adams said, in 1873, "One single hour of the will displayed by General Jackson would have stifled the fire in its cradle." The metaphor in the last phrase is peculiar, and strangely Celtic for a Yankee, but the history is true.

Montgomery Blair expressed the idea with greater plainness and vividness in that same year, 1873, in these words, "If we could have held Fort Sumter, there never would have been a drop of blood shed." Both these remarks were made by men who had been in some sense actors in the events to which they referred, and made after years of reflection upon the circumstances.

It does not seem to Americans of the present generation that there was ever a moment, after the election of Abraham Lincoln, when the Civil War could have been averted. It appears, in retrospect, to have been absolutely inevitable. Yet there was certainly one moment when, if President Buchanan had had the courage to apply the general views which he himself advanced in his annual message to Congress of December 3, 1860, and his special message of January 8, 1861, which explicitly denied the right of secession, a halt might have been called to the growing rebellion.

The secession movement was at first concentrated in the State of South Carolina. That State, all through the winter of 1860-1861, was presenting to the rest of the South an object lesson of successful nullification.

In 1833 South Carolina had ordained nullification, but its ordinance was so instantly and heavily repressed by President Andrew Jackson that the State was absolutely unable to carry it out, or to move hand or foot. But now, in 1860, it did not merely ordain nullification—it enacted it. Every Federal judge, every judicial servant, and nearly every Federal official, in South Carolina, resigned, and the nation was left without an agent to enforce its laws, for no new ones were sent in. The United States authority in the State was at an end, save for the custom house at Charleston and Fort Moultrie in Charleston harbor.

As long as South Carolina was let alone, her case plainly said to all the other slave States, "You see we can withdraw from the Union; we have withdrawn from the Union; and the Union takes no step to keep us in; you can do the same thing."

At this time North Carolina and Virginia were opposed to secession. Governor Sam Houston, of Texas, stood like a rock against it. Kentucky, Maryland, Missouri, never seceded. Other States were wavering. A great deal depended on the degree of success which South Carolina, the leader in the revolt, might have. And it was Buchanan who permitted South Carolina's success to become apparently complete, though in the message to which I have referred the president declared that secession was "wholly inconsistent with the Constitution," that "no human power could absolve him (the president) from his duty to enforce the laws," and that the danger of national disruption was upon the country. Buchanan, in his December message, actually quoted Jackson's solemn denunciation of the doctrine that a State had a right to separate itself from the Union.

But while he was making these terrible admissions of his own duty, what was Buchanan doing? Instead of holding up the hands of the nation's representatives in South Carolina, he was weakening them. Instead of strengthening the Federal garrison in Charleston harbor, he permitted it to dwindle until it was powerless to take a single step. Not one act, indeed, did he perform, but contented himself with calling on Congress for legislation to meet the emergency. And out of Congress, of course, he could get nothing, for the Southern representatives would vote for no such legislation, and the Republican members were bent upon waiting until Lincoln, who had been elected president, came in in March, and the northern Democrats were paralyzed with pusillanimity.

So South Carolina went on proving to the other slave States that it could "go it alone." One after another these other States seceded from the Union. Northern arsenals were stripped of arms. Southern officers went out of the army one by one, and made ready to organize the army of the new Confederacy which was forming under the president's nose.

It was a time for the strong arm, and for quick, decisive, Jacksonian, and not at all squeamish, action. But no such action was taken. The golden moment was lost, and when, three months afterward, Lincoln came in at last, war, with all its horrors, was upon the country.

If the young rebellion had been truly nipped in the bud, as it might have been, by a rigid enforcement, in November and December, 1860, of Federal judicial processes in South Carolina; if the laws of the United States had been enforced in that State at the point of the bayonet, if need be; if a Federal functionary, sustained by an ample force of United States troops, had torn South Carolina's ordinance of secession into shreds on the steps of the capitol at Columbia, with no tender regard for South Carolina's interpretation of the Constitution, is it likely that South Carolina's sister States would have been so prompt at seceding?

Very likely it might not have been necessary to do any of these things. If Buchanan had merely stood up and said, as Jackson did in 1833, "I shall enforce the laws of the United States in spite of any and all resistance that may be made," there might well have been no more of secession in 1860 or 1861 than there had been of real nullification in 1833.

And if this step had been taken, and there had been no war, what then? What about slavery? it may be asked. Is it conceivable that northern sentiment would have permitted chattel slavery to continue? Was not war inevitable on that main question alone? Let us see. The sentiment for absolute and sudden emancipation was the product of the war. Lincoln was not an Abolitionist. The Republican party was not Abolitionist.

Without war, but with the Southern States held within the Union, sentiment in the North would have been favorable to a compromise which would have prevented the extension of slavery; and events would surely have brought about a gradual liberation of the blacks in the South, as events soon ended slavery in Brazil and Cuba. The institution was doomed, morally and economically.

But there would have been no negro suffrage. That was enforced by conditions which grew out of the war. The South would not have been impoverished, and it could have afforded a gradual education of the negro in such a way as to fit him for free industry, and, in a limited way, for the exercise of the suffrage. There would have been no disturbing reversal of the position of the two races, to be followed by a violent restoration of white supremacy and an accompanying development of inveterate hostility between whites and blacks. The sections would not have drifted apart in industrial conditions and social constitution as they did under the influence of the war; we should not have had, perhaps, a money-mad North to counterbalance a ruined, desolated, disheartened South.

And where, at Antietam, at Gettysburg, at Fredericksburg, at Chattanooga, and on many humbler fields, the flags wave over the even ranks of myriads of soldier graves, the mocking-birds would sing in thickets which the bullet's hiss and the shriek of the shell had never profaned, while their teeming populations of dead men would either be alive today or entombed among their loved ones after lives of peaceful usefulness.

CHAPTER XXI
IF THE CONFEDERATES HAD MARCHED
ON WASHINGTON AFTER BULL RUN

There have been a great many attempts to excuse or minimize the failure of General Joseph E. Johnston to follow up the tremendous Confederate victory won by his second in command, General G. T. Beauregard, at Bull Run, July 21, 1861. That the Federal army was beaten literally to a pulp there can be no doubt. General Irwin McDowell, who commanded the Union forces, officially reported, after the battle, that all his troops were in flight "in a state of utter disorganization." "They could not," he wired on July 22d, "be prepared for action by tomorrow morning even were they willing. The larger part of the men are a confused mob, entirely demoralized." They were actually running away in such a state of panic that they could not get away, for commissary and ammunition wagons, congressmen's and other spectators' horses and carriages, artillery and sutlers' wagons were blocking the road, and panic stricken soldiers were falling over one another. When General McClellan came to take command after McDowell had been superseded, he reported this state of affairs: "I found no army to command—a mere collection of regiments cowering on the banks of the Potomac, some perfectly raw, others dispirited by defeat."

The Ifs of History

To reach the spot where the beaten raw recruits were thus cowering, General Johnston and General Beauregard had to advance only twenty miles, over a road every foot of which was well known to them. That the Federal army was in ignominious flight they were well aware, for they reported it joyfully to the government at Richmond. Why did they settle down into utter inaction and allow McClellan to fortify the capital and organize, drill and inspire with hope and confidence a great army?

There are a good many "ifs" in connection with the actual fighting of the battle of Bull Run, but this "if" that comes after it—if the elated and triumphant Confederate army had immediately advanced to the Potomac, invested the entrenchments at Arlington Heights and, very likely, effected a crossing above or near the Great Falls of the river, and flanked the capital of the Union—is the greatest and most interesting of them all.

General Beauregard actually commanded at the battle on the 21st, because General Johnston, who ranked him, had but just arrived on the scene and was unfamiliar with the ground and the disposition of the troops. But he, Johnston, became responsible for the further prosecution of the campaign, once the battle was won. It was in large measure his fault that the fruits of victory were not reaped.

The commonly accepted explanation of the matter is that the Confederates were "almost as much disorganized by victory as the Federals were by defeat;" that they had no fresh troops and no cavalry with which to pursue, and that Arlington Heights were too well fortified to be attacked.

But General Beauregard, sore at the attempt to rob him of the laurels of victory, has been able to show that all of the Confederate brigades of Ewell, Holmes, D. R. Jones and Longstreet, and two regiments of Bonham's brigade, were perfectly fresh and unharmed after the fight; that Early's brigade had hardly been under fire; that new regiments had come up during the day; that the fresh troops in all numbered at least fifteen thousand; that more than half the Confederate army, in fact, had not been engaged—a very unusual proportion after an important battle. "The remaining forces, after a night's rest," says Beauregard himself, "would have been instantly reorganized and found thoroughly safe to join the advance."

Apparently nothing but shame on the Northern side, and an unwillingness on the Southern side to discredit their great generals, has prevented a full acknowledgment of the fatal tactics which prevented an advance on the Potomac after Bull Run.

Now let us see what would have resulted from a Confederate investment of Washington in the summer of 1861. Federal troops had already been attacked in the streets of Baltimore. That city was preponderantly disloyal, and had to be garrisoned with Union troops. Missouri had not yet been won to the Union. Maryland, Delaware and Kentucky, all of which were necessary to the maintenance of the Northern position, were slave States, and their loyalty was doubtful. If the capital of the Union had been taken, all these States, in spite of their previous unwillingness to join the secession movement, would probably have been impelled by strong self-interest to range themselves on the side of the other slave States; and the Confederacy would have been strengthened by the addition of at least four States.

There was an important party among the Confederates from the western Southern States—it was led by Postmaster-General John H. Reagan and included General Albert Sidney Johnston—who believed in advancing at the very outset into Kentucky and making the Ohio River the first line of Southern defense. The plan was rejected by Davis and his advisers. It was an unfortunate rejection. The Confederacy was finally beaten because it was flanked in the west and cut in two at Vicksburg. But if Washington had been captured or invested after Bull Run, it is certain that the Confederate line would have been pushed to the Ohio, and it would probably have been held there. The advantage gained by McClellan in West Virginia would have been lost, for he would practically have found himself within the Confederate lines and would have been compelled to withdraw into Pennsylvania.

Even as matters were, the position of the Union was highly precarious all through the summer and autumn of 1861. There were signs of a demand for peace in the North. Lincoln's own party was turning against him. The sympathy of Europe was rapidly passing over to the Confederacy. But so long as Lincoln stood firm in the White House and Congress sat at the capital, "the government at Washington still lived," and the people felt it. The truce so kindly, so inexplicably permitted by Davis and Lee and Johnston enabled McClellan to organize and drill a great army, to fortify the capital, to spread renewed confidence in the North, and, in short, to establish a fulcrum for future victory.

This was not the last time that opportunity knocked at the door of the Confederacy. It knocked again, and loudly, as will be shown in the next chapter, the same year. Either event, taken alone, appears decisive. For as we contemplate the events of the 21st of July, 1861, it quite appears as if the flag of two republics—three, perhaps, and conceivably four—might have been flying over this great American domain to-day if Johnston had pressed his advance down the Warrenton turnpike early Monday morning, July 22d. Wars, divisions, European intrusion, retrogression and darkness would have been America's fate, instead of that imperial advance, with liberty and union, which has dazzled and heartened the whole world.

CHAPTER XXII
IF THE CONFEDERATE STATES HAD PURCHASED THE EAST INDIA COMPANY'S FLEET IN 1861

In the preceding chapter I have noted the disastrous consequences of the rejection of John H. Reagan's plan, urged at Montgomery at the very foundation of the Confederacy, for the prompt occupation of the south bank of the Ohio River as the advanced line of defense, and the equally unfavorable result of the failure of Johnston to press on to the Potomac after the great success at Manassas. Gettysburg was a pivotal combat, also; for if Lee had been supported by Stuart's cavalry on that occasion, there is at least a possibility that the war's tide might have been turned then and there.

But there was a narrower contingency than either one of these. To a positively decisive extent, the success of the National forces in subjugating the Southern States turned on the sea power. The conquest of the Confederacy was in fact a matter of supreme difficulty as it was; and if the South had possessed a respectable navy, and had been able to keep its ports open and steadily exchange its cotton in Europe for the materials and munitions of war, the conquest would not have been possible at all.

The chance for the establishment of such a navy lay within the grasp of the Confederate statesmen, and was by them let slip. Neither they, nor any one else at the time, realized how easy the thing would have been.

It is first necessary to explain in what situation the National government was, at the outset of the war, in the matter of a naval force. Nominally the United States navy consisted of ninety vessels, but of these fifty were utterly obsolete and unusable except as supply ships. Of the other forty, twenty were in a state of hopeless unreadiness. Several of the best ships were in the remotest corners of the world. The home squadron was composed of twelve ships, of which only seven were steamers! Nearly fifty years after the invention of steam navigation, the United States depended principally upon sailing vessels for its defense. Only three trustworthy warships were left in Northern waters for the defense of such ports as New York, Boston and Philadelphia.

As between the North and the South, the chance to wield the sea power lay with the one of the two rival governments which should first put on the water even a very small fleet of ironclad, steam-driven vessels. The Confederacy proved afterward what power could be exerted in this direction with but one single ironclad, when the *Merrimac* destroyed or scattered all the ships in Hampton Roads, for a moment threatened Washington and the Northern cities with ravage, and was checked at last only by the almost providential appearance of another ironclad, Ericsson's little *Monitor*, on the scene. And the *Alabama's* armor of chains made her for a time almost a match for the United States Navy.

By what means could the Confederacy have forestalled the North in the provision of a really effective navy? The chance, as I have said, was offered, and declined, with fatal want of foresight. It lay in the ten steamships of the English East India Company, which in 1861 was winding up its affairs. These ships were offered to the Confederacy at a fair valuation. They were very good vessels, and capable of prompt armoring in at least as effective a style as that in which the *Alabama* was afterwards armored. The East India

Company was prepared to make such terms as the Confederate government could have met.

British outfitters were perfectly willing to trust the Southern statesmen. The ships could have been armed in a few weeks; there was nothing to prevent their entrance into Southern ports, for the blockade was not made effective until one year after the war broke out. The *Otero*, renamed by the Confederates the *Florida*, had no difficulty in taking on her men and guns in the Bahamas.

Possessed of ten good steam vessels, commanded by such men as Maury, Maffitt of the *Florida*, and Semmes of the *Alabama*, the Confederacy could have quickly overcome its lack of mechanics and workshops by importation from Europe. It was the command of the Mississippi, the Cumberland and the Tennessee rivers which "broke the back of the Confederacy"; and does any one imagine that the wooden ships of Farragut could have entered the Mississippi, compelled the abandonment of New Orleans, and secured the possession of not only the seacoast but the inland river waters which commanded the Confederacy from the rear, if there had been any good ships to resist him?

The start which these ten ships would have given a Confederate navy would have more than put the South even with the North on the sea. It must be remembered that up to 1862, even as it was, the South could do better in the courts and exchanges of Europe than the Union could. Why? Because the South had the cotton, upon which the mills of Europe depended. The continued chance to market cotton would have saved the situation for the South. *Alabamas* in any requisite number would have issued from British shipyards.

As it was, several powerful rams were under construction for the Confederacy in 1861 and 1862 in the yards of the Lairds. But the continued insistence of Minister Adams on the unlawfulness of this proceeding, joined with the fact that the Confederates had no recognizable navy to back up their purchases, at last compelled the British government to take these rams over and add them to its own sea power.

President Jefferson Davis declined the offer of the East India ships for the apparent reason that the military necessities of the Confederacy pressed hard upon the financial resources of the new government. Every member of his government was quite thoroughly convinced that the National power could not successfully invade the South, provided a strong army were quickly put into the field. The ready material for good soldiers was much more abundant in the South than in the North; nearly all Southern men were horsemen, hunters, marksmen, out-of-door men. On the other hand, the first levies from the North were mostly city men, unaccustomed to firearms, strangers to exposure, flabby of physique. Manassas amply illustrated the great superiority as soldiers of the first comers from the South over the first comers from the North.

The Confederate leaders counted upon making permanent the advantage which they were confident of gaining in the field at the outset. To purchase out of hand ten steamships, from resources that were yet to be created, and with the manhood of seven States demanding to be armed, looked, indeed, like madness. And yet this was the very card which, if played, would have saved the Confederacy's game.

Conceive for a moment the Union navy debarred from entrance into the James or any of the navigable waters of Virginia, to support military operations in the direction of Richmond. Conceive Wilmington, N. C., which was an easily defensible port, and which really remained open to the blockade runners for almost two years after the beginning of the war, rendered a fairly safe point of departure for European trade throughout the war. Conceive the Mississippi, from Cairo southward to its mouth, continuously under the power of the Confederacy, with a fleet of river gunboats backed up by a Gulf squadron. Does any one imagine that in that case the North could have made either any warlike or commercial use of the Ohio, the Cumberland, the Tennessee, or even the Mississippi from Cairo up to St. Louis?

Freed from the unceasing coast menace and from the danger of being cut in two along the rivers, the effectiveness of the land forces would have been more than doubled. Leaving out of the account the possibility of offensive operations against Washington and the cities of the North, the defense of the seceded States could have been made so secure that the people of the North would have called loudly for peace; the border slave States would have cast in their lot with the Confederacy, and England and France would have openly sided with the South; secession would have triumphed definitely before the end of the year 1863.

With the English East India Company, it was a case of "take our ships or leave them." The South left them, and with them it left its chance for independence and for putting two mediocre American republics in the place where one great one, after that decisive moment, was bound to stand forever.

**For the Finest in
Nautical and Historical
Fiction and Nonfiction**

www.FireshipPress.com

Interesting • Informative • Authoritative

Lightning Source UK Ltd.
Milton Keynes UK
UKOW04f0617130813

215278UK00003B/283/P